BUILDING FAITH

Strengthening Your Love
for God, Others, and Yourself

BUILDING
Faith

REBECCA NOLTING

ASK PUBLISHING
Pueblo, Colorado

Building Faith: Strengthening Your Love for God, Others, and Yourself

Copyright © 2024 by Rebecca Nolting
All rights reserved.

No part of this work may be reproduced or transmitted in any form or by any means, electronic or mechanical, including photocopying and recording, or by any information storage or retrieval system, except as may be expressly permitted by the 1976 Copyright Act or in writing from the publisher. Requests for permission can be emailed to rebecca@extraordinaryfromordinary.com.

ASK Publishing books may be purchased in bulk at special discounts for sales promotion, corporate gifts, and ministry, fundraising, or educational purposes. Special editions can also be created to specifications. For details, contact rebecca@extraordinaryfromordinary.com.

Unless otherwise marked, scripture quotations are taken from THE HOLY BIBLE, NEW INTERNATIONAL VERSION®, NIV® Copyright © 1973, 1978, 1984, 2011 by Biblica, Inc.® Used by permission. All rights reserved worldwide.

Scripture quotations marked NLT are taken from the *Holy Bible*, New Living Translation, copyright © 1996, 2004, 2015 by Tyndale House Foundation. Used by permission of Tyndale House Publishers, Inc., Carol Stream, Illinois 60188. All rights reserved.

Scripture quotations marked NRSV are taken from the New Revised Standard Version Bible, copyright © 1989, by the Division of Christian Education of the National Council of the Churches of Christ in the U.S.A., and are used by permission. All rights reserved.
Visit our website at www.extraordinaryfromordinary.com.

ISBN softcover: 978-1-7376370-2-8
ISBN E-book: 978-1-7376370-3-5

Library of Congress Control Number: 202490128

Cover and interior design by Marisa Jackson for TLC Book Design, TLCBookDesign.com.

To those who battle mental health struggles every day, you are seen and loved.

TABLE OF CONTENTS

Acknowledgments	ix
Letter from the Author	xi

PART ONE *Preparing* 1

- *one* **Building Time** — 3
- *two* **Location, Location, Location** — 9
- *three* **Faithful in God's Plan** — 15
- *four* **What's Your Strategy for Learning?** — 23
- *five* **Measure Twice** — 29

PART TWO *Building* 35

- *six* **Foundationally Built** — 37
- *seven* **Grace-Filled Wood** — 45
- *eight* **Framework of Prayer** — 53
- *nine* **Roof of Trust and Protection** — 59
- *ten* **Wired in Loving Yourself** — 65
- *eleven* **Insulating Ourselves with Scripture** — 73

twelve	Solid Wall of Believers	79
thirteen	Colorful Suffering	85
fourteen	Walking in Faith	91
fifteen	Furnishing Refuge	97

PART THREE *Living* — 103

sixteen	Who Is Invited to Come In?	105
seventeen	Delays or God's Timing?	111
eighteen	Growing Faith	117
nineteen	Glad to Be Home!	123

ACKNOWLEDGMENTS

First, I want to praise God for being my solid foundation. I am so thankful for his grace and mercy and love in all my moments, especially the darkest ones.

Second, I want to thank my husband, Jeffrey, for being my rock since we met in 2004. Words cannot fully express what his love during my mental health struggles has meant to me.

Third, thank you to Pastor Scott Schurle for not only agreeing to read my drafts again, but also for offering the guidance and encouragement I needed to "keep chopping."

Next, the amazing team at TLC Book Design—Tamara, Misti, and Marisa—has helped me immensely to continue my dream of being a writer.

Thanks also to the countless people who helped guide me on my faith journey, including family, friends, and church leaders who have shown me the love of Jesus.

Finally, thank you to the people who have shown me I am loved, supported, and not alone in this journey of life.

LETTER FROM THE AUTHOR

Dear Friend,

Back in 2020, while in Bible study, my pastor (Scott) kept using the word "foundation." As he said it for the third or fourth time, I heard God whisper the idea for this book. A proper foundation is key for a house, but it is also important in your faith journey. I started seeing similarities between building a house and building one's faith. They both require taking it step-by-step and making a commitment. There are many decisions that will test your patience and commitment on your walk with God. As your life progresses, you can see how your faith has evolved and the lessons learned. The idea of viewing ourselves as a living house isn't new, as C.S. Lewis wrote:

> Imagine yourself as a living house. God comes in to rebuild that house. At first, perhaps, you can understand

what He is doing. He is getting the drains right and stopping the leaks in the roof and so on: you knew that those jobs needed doing and so you are not surprised. But presently He starts knocking the house about in a way that hurts abominably and does not seem to make sense. What on earth is He up to? The explanation is that He is building quite a different house from the one you thought of—throwing out a new wing here, putting on an extra floor there, running up towers, making courtyards. You thought you were going to be made into a decent little cottage: but He is building a palace. He intends to come and live in it Himself.[1]

One of the big themes of this book is love because that is what Jesus's ministry revolves around. When Jesus was asked what the greatest commandment was, "Jesus replied, 'Love the Lord your God with all your heart and with all your soul and with all your mind. This is the first and greatest commandment. And the second is like it: Love your neighbor as yourself. All the Law and the Prophets hang on these two commandments'" (Matthew 22:37–40). My goal is to show examples of love from the Bible and in my own life.

It also seemed natural to me to talk about construction. My dad was an engineer and designed many buildings in his

---

[1] C. S. Lewis, *Mere Christianity*, New York: Touchstone, 1996, p. 176.

life. My husband, Jeffrey, helped many times in his dad's construction business and has worked on almost every aspect of building a home. Our current home has an addition and garage built by him and his family, and I have been able to help with many renovation projects. While I did learn a lot about the building process while writing this book, I am by no means an expert or someone to look to for building advice. (My husband requested that I put this disclaimer in!)

At the end of each chapter, there are reflection questions to use as journal prompts or in a discussion group. It also includes a building challenge. This is because we are called to have an active faith. I have also included a song at the end of each chapter for you to listen to because music is another way to connect with God. The songs chosen helped inspire me on my faith journey. Use these songs to worship God, as a way to pray, or both!

Let's get started building our faith!

Rebecca

BRIDGE

CASTING CROWNS

PART ONE
Preparing

one

BUILDING TIME

For everything there is a season, and a time for every matter under heaven ... a time to break down, and a time to build up.

ECCLESIASTES 3:1, 3 (NRSV)

DECONDITIONED is the word my chiropractor used a few years ago to describe my healing from a car accident. Even though I had been doing the stretches and going for walks, it wasn't enough to heal quickly. I wasn't fully committed, and it showed. I also had lost the habit of going for walks regularly, so the result wasn't surprising.

You can be deconditioned in all areas of your life, not just physically. It can be mentally, emotionally, or spiritually as well. It can also include not having built up the skills, abilities, and knowledge strong enough in the first place. "Deconditioning is a complex process of physiological change following a period of inactivity, bedrest or sedentary lifestyle."[1] Hearing that word, deconditioned, motivated me, both mentally and physically, to pursue the healing that I wanted. It took many walks and stretches to get my back to the point where I had no more pain. Having the desire to improve is important, but I had to be willing to commit my time. I have to continually commit to maintaining and improving my overall health.

Building a house starts with learning where to begin. For example, you can't paint walls before putting up sheetrock or put on a roof before framing is complete. Building takes a lot of time and commitment because it can feel like a painfully slow process some days. It's not something that happens overnight or that you can stop halfway through for the results you want. I have never built a house from the foundation myself. I also had never written a book prior to 2021, but here I am, writing my second book. My point is just because you have never done something doesn't mean that you can't learn. When you decided to believe in Jesus, you didn't have all the knowledge or skills. You just knew you wanted to start your walk with Jesus. But where do you start? Do you just start reading the Bible? Many people, like myself, have read Scripture without understanding

---

[1] Angela Gillis and Brenda MacDonald, "Deconditioning in the hospitalized elderly," *Can Nurse*, National Library of Medicine, National Center for Biotechnology Information, June 2005, https://pubmed.ncbi.nlm.nih.gov/16121472/.

the history or context. The words can be comforting, but other times, they can be confusing or even overwhelming.

This is why it is important to develop your own routine to condition, or re-condition, yourself to read the Bible, pray, and seek God in every situation. Developing a new routine takes time, commitment, and motivation. This also means applying what you have learned. Jesus showed us that the answer to any question of what do to is love: Love God, love your neighbor, and love yourself. (Loving yourself includes taking care of yourself, not loving self over God.) But how do we show love? Fred Rodgers gives us this answer: "Love isn't a state of perfect caring. It is an active noun like struggle. To love someone is to strive to accept that person exactly the way he or she is, here and now."[2] That's where the practice of showing love, even if, or especially when, you don't feel like it, can build your faith.

When I started to brainstorm for this book, I realized that I couldn't use the same stories that I had in my first book. What better way to build my faith than to push myself to take the time to learn about different Bible stories and people? As I sat, stumped as to which story to pick for this first chapter, I went to the back of our Bible to the index. This has the list of Bible subjects, which includes the people in the Bible. The first

---

[2] Fred Rogers, "Love isn't a state of perfect caring," AZ Quotes, accessed on December 23, 2023, https://www.azquotes.com/quote/390332.

one, naturally, was Aaron. I realized I didn't know much about Aaron, so I started reading the referenced Scriptures. It was fun for me to learn new things, and I was just on my first word.

A few things I learned about Aaron include how important Aaron's role was during the exodus from Egypt. I knew he was Moses's brother, but he was right there with Moses on many of the pleas to release the Israelites. He was also there for almost the entire time they were wandering in the desert. Along with Moses, Aaron also wasn't allowed into the Promised Land because of his disobedience. Even though Aaron and Moses had seen God come through time after time, when it came to fully showing their trust in God, they fell short. "But the LORD said to Moses and Aaron, 'Because you did not trust in me enough to honor me as holy in the sight of the Israelites, you will not bring this community into the land I give them'" (Numbers 20:12). God didn't stop loving them, but there were consequences for their lack of trust. It can be a challenge to always be obedient in your faith walk.

Aaron also had a few other blunders before this, including the famous golden calf story. Moses went up to the mountain to receive the Law from God, and the people were grumbling about how long it was taking. (Sound familiar? We never grumble about how long something is taking, do we?) Aaron was talked into making gods out of their gold. His response to Moses was not the best: "'Do not be angry, my Lord', Aaron answered. 'You know how prone these people are to evil....

Then they gave me the gold, and I threw it into the fire, and out came this calf!'" (Exodus 32:22, 24). He put the blame on the people and the fire. It can feel easier to point the finger at anyone or anything else than take responsibility for our own actions. God was upset and was ready to kill Aaron for it. But thanks to his brother, Moses, interceding, God didn't. I am thankful that even though Aaron messed up multiple times (He was human!), God is merciful. It gives me hope that I can slip up, but if I repent, I can receive God's forgiveness.

Even though God did not allow Aaron into the Promised Land, God did keep his promise to Aaron and his family to make them priests. As high priests, they were mediators between the people and God. Their lives were dedicated to the Lord, and they relied on the other tribes to support them. Nowadays, we can recognize this role in Catholic priests. I was raised Catholic and see many similarities to the first priests, including going to confession in which the priests serve as an intercessory to God.

The writers of the Bible describe God in four ways: Priest (intercessor), Elohim (creator), Jehovah "Yahweh" (personable), and Deuteronomy (One you worship). As you read the Bible and build your faith, you can see the different aspects of God come through. You can feel the awe of the Creator in some passages while also seeing the personable aspect of God who wants to help us in other passages. We can also see the importance of worshipping both in our hearts and at the altar. Each is important to strengthen your relationship with God.

When we reviewed these aspects of God in a Bible study, I realized I viewed God through a priest perspective. I didn't feel comfortable going straight to God to build a relationship and am still working on my discomfort. You may have had a similar experience where God felt distant, like you can only communicate through priests. But the good news is, you can find ways to build that muscle through prayer and reading the Bible. Every relationship takes work, and God welcomes all efforts.

When you start a new project or commit more fully to it, it's important to keep going and keep trying. No matter how slow a pace, every step builds your faith, if you give it time.

REFLECTION QUESTIONS:
1. *How would you describe where you are in your faith journey right now?*
2. *How can each of the aspects of God build your faith?*

BUILDING CHALLENGE

Write out one goal for your life and steps it will take to achieve it. Do step one.

two

LOCATION, LOCATION, LOCATION

**The wise woman builds her house,
but with her own hands the
foolish one tears hers down.**

PROVERBS 14:1

THE SECOND STEP is to decide where you want to build, or rebuild, your house. To help with that decision, you need to determine how much space you'll need for the house, garage, and yard. It may mean making a difficult decision to move to a whole new location, far away from what you know. When it comes to building our faith, you may also have to give up old beliefs or activities to make room for new ones.

When I think about going to a foreign place without knowing what to expect, the biblical story of Ruth comes to mind. She married a man whose family was originally from Bethlehem. The family had moved to Moab because of a famine in Judah. Unfortunately, Ruth's husband died, along with her father-in-law and brother-in-law. All she had left were her mother-in-law, Naomi, and her sister-in-law, Orpah. "When Naomi heard in Moab that the LORD had come to the aid of his people by providing food for them, she and her daughters-in-law prepared to return home from there" (Ruth 1:6). For Naomi, the decision to move back to Bethlehem was not difficult to make because she could go home.

Naomi recognized the risk Ruth and Orpah faced if they went with her: They might remain widows. She showed her love to her daughters-in-law by releasing their obligations to her. Orpah chose to return to her family, but Ruth chose Naomi, Naomi's God, and an unknown journey. Ruth also chose to leave behind her old beliefs, which made space for believing in Naomi's God. Bethlehem is where she met Boaz, who was Naomi's relative. Boaz became Naomi's kinsman redeemer and restored her family name. A true act of *khesed*, which means "unconditional love, generosity, and enduring commitment."[1] This story of deciding to build their lives back in Bethlehem had lasting effects: King David and Jesus are in Ruth's family line. We also may not know the impact of our decisions in our lifetime.

---

[1] "Loyal Love," Bible Project, accessed on November 5, 2023, https://bibleproject.com/explore/video/loyal-love/.

If Bethlehem sounds familiar, it is also where Jesus was born. Why did Mary and Joseph travel to Bethlehem for the required census? "So Joseph also went up from the town of Nazareth in Galilee to Judea, to Bethlehem the town of David, because he belonged to the house and line of David" (Luke 2:4). Bethlehem means house of bread. How fitting is it that the bread of life took his first breaths in Bethlehem? Once again, the actions of one generation, Joseph and Mary, had an impact on the future. Eternally even.

When I think about my own life, I can look at my move to Colorado in a similar way Ruth did hers to Bethlehem. I chose to move there without checking it out to be sure it was what I wanted. My field supervisor had attended the University of Denver and was pleased with her experience. Ruth trusted Naomi, as I trusted my supervisor in making the decision to go. I took the leap, believing it was where I was meant to go. Like Ruth, it is where I met my husband. Once I finished my master's program, I believed it was the right relationship, so I chose to move to Pueblo to be with him. It felt like Naomi's decision: easy. It was what I wanted and needed—a place to feel at home. Since my husband was established in his home, we made the decision for me to move in. These steps into the unknown have built my faith by giving me the peace that comes with the right decision. We can use Ruth's story to inspire us to believe that if we seek God in our decisions, he will lead us to where we are meant to be.

One project that we worked on was a new shed. (Well, he did most of the work and I encouraged him.) He started building a shed out of pallets he got from his workplace with the intent to sell it. As it started taking shape, I liked it more and more. I asked, "Can we keep it and tear down our old one?" He was for it, and as a result, new plans were made. We started the new shed, but reached a tipping point where the old shed had to be torn down so we could finish the new one. One of my jobs was to organize the items we wanted to keep in the transitional time. I liked that part—throwing away old things, recycling some things, giving some things to a family member, and keeping only what we needed. It felt like a fresh start, which we may want in areas of our lives.

Sometimes, a fresh start or big change is not what we want, but it's what we need. It can be turning from sin and old habits when you chose to accept Christ. It can also be making a difficult decision that changes your life forever. I faced a challenging decision soon after I published my first book. It was on Thanksgiving 2021 when I heard a whisper, "It's time to give up Worship Chair." A peace came over me. I had been in that position for six years, and like our old shed, it was a fixture in my life. The business side of selling books was more work than I realized. Following my dream of being an author was taking time away from my church responsibilities. It was extremely tough and frustrating to navigate the balance between the two. I tried announcing that I would stay on for one more year. My frustrations kept growing, and it felt like I had no choice but to resign much sooner.

Looking back, it felt like God was telling me, "Yes, I told you to give that up, and I didn't mean later. I meant now." There were many factors in the decision, but it was like when Ruth was given a choice to go, stay still, or move forward. She had to make a decision and stick with it. I chose to listen to God and step down. We don't read about the grief process Ruth must have gone through as she literally walked away from the world she knew. But I can relate to the feelings of loss, and you probably can as well. It does take believing that there is something greater in store. Like Paul said in Romans 8:28, "And we know that in all things God works for the good of those who love him, who have been called according to his purpose." Ruth and my own examples show our love for and trust in God.

Ruth left her old life to follow Naomi and Naomi's God. Because Ruth said yes to a new location and listened to Naomi's wise instructions, she was one of the only women listed in the genealogy of Jesus in the book of Matthew. We don't get all the steps of faith laid out for us ahead of time, but you can build your faith in each and every decision you make.

REFLECTION QUESTIONS:
1. *How can you show others God's love in the location you are in?*
2. *What is one old belief or activity that you may need to tear down to make room for something new?*

BUILDING CHALLENGE

Where will your faith take you? Pray that God will show you, and you will be willing to go.

three

FAITHFUL IN GOD'S PLAN

> "For I know the plans I have for you," declares the LORD, "plans to prosper you and not to harm you, plans to give you hope and a future."
>
> JEREMIAH 29:11

ONCE YOU FIGURE out where you are going to build, you need a plan for the house. This includes a blueprint for the builders. Are you going to go with the now popular open floor plan or make unique choices for the layout? These key decisions will affect all the other plans and decisions you make. How have you let your faith guide you in your plans, including unexpected ones, in your life?

One of the popular concepts in house design is flow. Does one room flow to the next? Or, to apply it to faith, how has your life flowed from one experience to another? When

I think about going with the flow and being faithful in it, I think of King David. He has been described as "a man after [God's] own heart" (1 Samuel 13:14). God told Samuel to go anoint another king and was guided to David. Can you imagine being told you were going to be king and then sent back to the fields to tend sheep? David must have been building his faith in God during that time because, a few years later, he was bold enough to take on Goliath with just his slingshot and his faith. "Faithfulness to God didn't start in an arena with Goliath and a crowd of spectators. It started alone, in the wilderness, with no one watching but God and a flock of sheep."[1]

But then, he wasn't appointed king for many more years. During that time, David showed faithfulness by building his relationship with God. What is confusing is how David, with all his faith, let his fleshly desires tempt him towards Bathsheba. He was even willing to have her husband killed to cover up his sins. What gives me hope is God knew all of David's weaknesses and still chose him to be king. He saw his heart. David showed his remorse when confronted by Nathan the prophet and took whatever consequences he was given. God had a plan, a blueprint, for David, but it was up

---

[1] Annie Stewart Lambert, "Faithfulness to God didn't start in an arena with Goliath and a crowd of spectators," Facebook, April 28, 2023, https://www.facebook.com/photo?fbid=10225931675771174&set =a.10200484424125787.

to David to follow through with it or not. God has a blueprint for us all as well, and we also have the choice to follow it or not. David made mistakes, but this gives us hope that if we recognize it and repent, we can return to God's plan.

When I mentioned about God telling me on Thanksgiving to give up Worship Team in the previous chapter, there was a piece I didn't share. That same day, I shared with my husband that I had been diagnosed with depression. He was supportive without knowing fully how to help me with it. His response was, "I figured that's what it was." It is something, in combination with anxiety, that I believe I battled with at different times in my life. With new and more intense stressors in my life, it came on more intensely.

Unfortunately, people have linked sin and mental/physical struggles for centuries. They believed that because you had a disability, you must have sinned. Or if it was a child, it was the parents' sin. This made the person who was struggling feel like if they just repented, then they would be healed. I can imagine this would have been frustrating if they tried to repent and it didn't work. In some ways, this type of judgment continues today. Sin is giving in to fleshly desires and not following God's will, while mental health struggles can include brain chemistry gone haywire. You can control when you sin, but you can't always fully control mental health on your own.

The next step is to find ways to work through mental health struggles. When you have depression and anxiety, it can be tempting to feel like you have no faith or that God has or will abandon you because of all your negative thoughts. Or that you have sinned because of the thoughts you have had. I have had to learn that these are lies and to fight them with the knowledge that God does love me. God knew that I would have this struggle, but still chose me. That is quite a powerful and overwhelming feeling!

One way I know God knew this part of my plan for my life is back when I was about two or three years old. It was the year that Care Bears were super popular for Christmas. All I asked for was Grumpy Bear. What a strange choice, right? It took a lot of work on my mom's part, with help from a friend, to get me and my sisters the Care Bears we wanted. I have no memory of actually having the bear, but I am told I had it with me a lot. More recently, while working through things in therapy, I thought of Grumpy Bear. I googled what his description was: "Grumpy Bear frowns a lot—that's his way to show us how silly we look when we frown too much. He also shows that it's okay to be grumpy sometimes. But even when we're grumpy, we're still loved."[2] Wow. If you insert the word depression, anxiety, or any other negative emotion, this means we are still loved. What amazes me is how I was shown this about forty years later. I ordered a new Grumpy Bear as a way

---

2   "Grumpy Bear," Care Bear Bios, accessed November 5, 2023, http://drifting_memories.tripod.com/id20.html.

to remind myself of God's love for me and how I need to love myself in those times as well. These kinds of tactile reminders help me get through tough moments.

My original theme of this chapter was about comparing ourselves when it comes to how our houses look. When I shared it with my pastor, his response was "metanoia," which means "to change one's mind"[3] in Greek or, in simpler terms, to think again. Metanoia is another way to describe repentance for our sins. I realized that talking about comparing ourselves to others isn't how we can build our faith, but rather, it's a distraction. We can compare our struggles to others, or even our successes, and not fulfill our specific blueprint. From the outside, it doesn't make sense that I would have depression, and I even heard someone ask, "What do you have to be depressed about?" I understand I have been blessed in many ways, but this diagnosis is a part of my specific blueprint, and not everyone will understand.

One of the ways people work through their struggles is through writing, and many people have turned their words into the most beautiful songs. Many contemporary Christian songs are about struggles, even using words like anxiety, depression, pain, and battles. But this is not a new concept, as many hymns were also written in times of anguish. One

---

3 Merriam Webster Online, s.v. "metanoia (n)," accessed January 10, 2024, https://www.merriam-webster.com/dictionary/metanoia.

popular song is "It Is Well with My Soul." The original words were written by H. G. Spafford. The story is that he wrote these words while he was traveling to meet his wife after his son had died, he had lost a lot of property to a fire, and his four daughters had drowned in a shipwreck. The words just flowed out during this excruciating time.

> When peace, like a river, attendeth my way,
> When sorrows, like a sea billows roll;
> Whatever my lot, Thou hast taught me to say,
> It is well, it is well with my soul.[4]

David also used music as a way to help him through his tough times. He was a musician and also wrote many of the psalms that are still used as a source of comfort. It can be a challenge to fully appreciate the words when you are in the depths of a struggle. What I found as I came out of the depression fog was that even though I felt alone, I wasn't. I could draw on many psalms and contemporary song lyrics to help me draw closer to God.

We also need to continually commit to the blueprint we have been given, with God's help. Are you going to go with the ebbs and flows of life, the good and the bad, with God or

---

[4] Mel Johnson, "The Story behind the Hymn 'It Is Well with My Soul," GodUpdates, March 7, 2016, https://www.godupdates.com/story-behind-it-is-well-with-my-soul/.

FAITHFUL IN GOD'S PLAN ✟ 21

without him? God sees the beginning and the end. He knew people would turn from him, but he still chose to save us.

If you think you have ruined the blueprint for your life, think again.

REFLECTION QUESTIONS:
1. Are you seeking God's blueprint for your life?
2. Is there a sin that you need to confess, to repent?

BUILDING CHALLENGE
Find your own tactile reminder that God loves you.

IT IS WELL WITH MY SOUL
H. G. SPAFFORD

four

WHAT'S YOUR STRATEGY FOR LEARNING?

> **All Scripture is God-breathed and is useful for teaching, rebuking, correcting and training in righteousness, so that the servant of God may be thoroughly equipped for every good work.**
>
> 2 TIMOTHY 3:16–17

One decision you need to make when building a house is whether you are going to do the work yourself (Do It Yourself), hire professionals for the various pieces, or a combination of both. When it comes to learning, do you try to do it all on your own, only rely on others to teach you, or a mixture of both? What tools are you using to help you learn?

One of the tools I am using to build my faith is learning where all the books of the Bible are. You can use tabs to help, but I choose to try to find the books on my own. The more I am in the Word and familiar with the order, the more appreciation I have developed for each story and how they tie together. As you read, you will notice the repetition of certain words, themes, instructions, and stories. I believe there is repetition because we need to hear things over and over for them to really penetrate into our souls. Like exercising our bodies, it's not just a one-and-done and we're in shape. It takes repetition to build muscles. I have seen that the more I read, the more I have been able to connect the stories. It also has pushed my inquisitive mind to explore more.

As part of my challenge, I decided I wanted to get a new Bible, so I researched the different versions of the Bible. Growing up Catholic, I was familiar with the King James Version, which, for me, was difficult to read. Some people like and use that version, which is great. What is wonderful is that there are so many to choose from now. I chose to stay with the NIV and use the *Quest Study Bible*. I liked the name because I was and still am on a quest to learn more. What I have enjoyed about this particular version is the questions and answers throughout. Many times, when I have read a verse and had a question about it, it's already been answered in the notes. It's reassuring that I was not alone in being confused about context or wanting a little more information. It's also helpful to compare a verse in different translations, so I also have a Bible app. Other study aids, like a Bible dictionary and commentaries, are great tools to help you understand a parable or give more history on a person.

Studying alone is only one part of any project. I have learned that when I want to tackle a home project, I should rely on other people who have done it before. I have no skills in drawing, but I still tried to draw some trees and a cabin on the side of a homemade trailer we had. Let's just say that I painted over the scene almost immediately because it looked horrible. If I had sought some advice from others more skilled in that area, it may have come out much better. Advice from others isn't limited to other Christians. God can talk to us through anyone, even an atheist. Advice from anyone should be checked against Scripture to make sure it doesn't contradict the written Word.

The day I was working on this chapter, I went to a local art gallery where I have copies of my first book. I told one of the artists, "I can appreciate the skills the artists have because I have none."

He responded, "People can have those skills deep down, but they need to be drawn out, and those people are probably the most talented."

I know this was an affirmation from God that I can achieve things I never thought I could, and you can as well. It was a good reminder to always be aware of what God can teach you through others at any given moment.

In addition to reading and studying the Bible on your own, it is also important to be part of a group Bible study. Someone else may have insight on a particular subject that helps you understand. What that also means is to be in Bible study with different groups of people. I was invited to a Bible study at a different church, and I was nervous because I didn't know the people and what to expect. I thought I was agreeing to a short study, but it turned out to be a thirty-four-lesson study. It was a blessing to me because it structured the readings in a new way and pushed me to learn.

I learned a funny lesson when I was given a used study manual, meaning I had someone else's notes. That was eye-opening because I was shown another perspective. One comment that spoke to me was, "Our obedience to God should not be assumed easy or come naturally."[1] This statement fits because of my discomfort with going to another church group's Bible study. But it was in stepping out in faith that I learned more about God, which helped strengthen my relationship with him.

God shows his love on every page of the Bible. What makes me appreciate that even more is that the Bible we hold in our hands today wasn't in the hands of the prophets, Jesus, or the first believers. We are spoiled to have access to all the versions, commentaries, social media posts, videos, and even movies based on Scripture. Or maybe it's to our detriment to have this

---

1   Anonymous comment, "Our obedience to God should not be assumed easy or come naturally," *Becoming Disciples Through Bible Study*, p. 26.

abundance. It can deter us from the basics and make us too reliant on others' interpretations.

One way to learn more about the Bible is through games, whether a competition to find a specific Scripture, trivia, or a game called "Chutes and Ladders." I know God has a good sense of humor with me because that seems like a random childhood game. But, in trying to be obedient, I looked up the origins of the game.

What I learned was there are other versions of the game that teach morality, and even one called "Bible Ups and Downs." The rules state that the goal is to get to Christ, and the way is through the Bible. That made sense to me, as there are many prophecies about Christ in the Old Testament. Even though it's just a childhood game, we can be inspired by the ups and downs in the Bible. I know it can feel like two steps forward, one step back (or slide down) in your faith journey. But be reassured that we all go through it, and the more you read the Bible, the more you can see you are not the first person to deal with certain struggles.

When it comes to building your faith, it is important to use the combination of DIY, group learning, and any other available tools. What is equally vital is being open to new ways of learning because that is when we are stretched. The key is: the more we read, the more we can see God's love. In all our studying, we will be doing a new building strategy: Do It with God (DIwG).

REFLECTION QUESTIONS:
1. What Bible version do you use and why?
2. How can you stretch your learning strategies?

BUILDING CHALLENGE

Find one of your favorite Scriptures to read in another version.

DO IT YOURSELF SONG

LISTEN TO A FAVORITE SONG OR FIND A NEW ONE THAT GIVES YOU ENCOURAGEMENT.

five MEASURE TWICE

> I don't deserve the 143,982 chances God has already given to me and I don't deserve any that He will give me in the future. But there He is, always by my side. Thank you Lord.[1]

ONE OF THE tips I have heard when doing any construction project is: Measure twice, cut once. The theory is that you are less likely to make a mistake if you double-check your work. Not fail-proof, but good practice. It's better to cut something too big than too small because you can fix it much easier. It is by making

---

[1] Servant Hearted Sisterhood, "I don't deserve the 143,982 chances God has already given me," Facebook, May 26, 2023, https://www.facebook.com/photo?fbid=269409235447480&set=a.192899579765113.

mistakes and learning from them that we build our faith. Then there are times when something looks like a mistake in the moment, but then God's glory shines through.

Before you measure, it's important to know what you need to measure. This is equally as important in cooking as in construction. One wrong move can result in a disgusting outcome. I learned the importance of properly measuring ingredients while making my mom's spaghetti sauce for the first time. I had eaten it many times and thought it was going to be fine because I had the recipe. What I didn't realize was I had changed it. When it said two cloves of garlic, I thought it was the whole thing, not two pieces of it. As I diced a lot of garlic, I didn't remember my mom taking that much time with the garlic.

But, instead of double-checking the measurement, in went the garlic into the sauce. Even though it wasn't supposed to have that much garlic, it wasn't disastrous. My mistake helped me to learn to check what the instructions meant and not assume that I knew. When we assume something about a person or situation, it can be a disaster. The result could be much worse than super garlicky spaghetti sauce; it could be ruined relationships. Thankfully, if we seek wisdom from God, we can mend relationships or at least learn what not to do next time.

It can also be tempting to spend too much time measuring and not trusting that you have it right. When I went on a mission trip to Kansas with my church, one of the tasks was to put up siding. We were separated into two groups. The group I joined didn't know much about putting up siding, but with quick instructions, we got to work. The other group had members who were more experienced but wouldn't trust what they had measured was right. They measured a piece several times before making a cut. They let fear of making a mistake slow down their progress. I bet you can guess which group finished first. The less experienced group probably made some mistakes, but our confidence grew as we worked. We were also willing to make mistakes and learn from them rather than not try at all. Less fear and more trust in God stretches and builds us.

We do need to be careful how we measure love from one another. I have struggled with perfectionism and felt that any mistake could cost me someone's love, even God's. Living with that fear made me second-guess myself when making decisions. I have been breaking that conditioning by seeing how God and others have loved me for who I am, not what I have accomplished. It can be tempting to be hard on ourselves for making mistakes in all areas of our lives, even in our faith journey. Some choices we make may feel like a mistake at the time. But, when we look back, mistakes, even perceived ones, are where we learn something about ourselves.

One story in the Bible that, on the surface, looked like a mistake was made was the story of Lazarus. Jesus knew his family well, but when he received a message that Lazarus was sick, he stayed where he was for two more days. When Jesus did show up, Martha was upset and told him, "Lord...if you had been here, my brother would not have died. But I know that even now God will give you whatever you ask" (John 11:21–22). I believe she thought Jesus had messed up (made a mistake by not coming sooner) but was trying to still have faith in Jesus. Mary also then shared her frustration at Jesus's absence. What happened next was the real reason for Jesus's delay. He went to Lazarus's tomb and called out his name after the men rolled away the stone. Out walked Lazarus—what a sight to see! Sometimes, what appears to man to be a mistake is meant to show God's glory instead.

Jesus's disciples also had warned him that returning to Judea for Lazarus would put him in a dangerous position, which they perceived would be a mistake. The Jewish leaders were already looking for reasons to have Jesus killed, and raising Lazarus from the dead was creating more fear. Their argument was that if more people believed in Jesus, it would attract attention from Rome. Then Rome would come take away their temple and nation, which meant their high standing positions would be gone as well. Their mistake was that they let their own fears take precedence. Or was it a mistake that they viewed the Messiah through human eyes only? God knew that the Jewish people perceived that the Messiah would save them from Rome. God utilized that knowledge to allow our Messiah to save us from something much bigger: our sins.

Two things stuck out for me in this story. First is the shortest verse in the Bible: "Jesus wept" (John 11:35). Even though he knew what he was going to do, he felt the human emotion of sadness. This gives me comfort that even though God wins in the end, he still feels heartache with us. That is one way that Jesus shows love for us: through empathizing with our struggles.

The second was how the chief priests were planning not only Jesus's demise, but also Lazarus's. "So the chief priests made plans to kill Lazarus as well, for on account of him many of the Jews were going over to Jesus and believing in him" (John 12:10–11). What a testimony Lazarus had to give! He was literally dead and was given a second chance at life. This story gives us this hope: We can never make a mistake too big for God to want to give us a second (or third or five hundredth) chance. He does love us more than all our mistakes.

How does making mistakes help build our faith? It's where we learn how to rely on God. We aren't perfect, but God is. We are all a work in progress, but we can remember to look to God more in every part in our lives. "And being found in appearance as a man, he humbled himself by becoming obedient to death—even death on a cross!" (Philippians 2:8). And remember:

> Sometimes we're so ashamed of ourselves that we automatically feel like Jesus is too. But He's not.

He knew you'd struggle, He knew you'd make some wrong decisions, He knew you'd go through some rough phases, but He still chose the cross. Don't run from Him. Run to Him.[2]

REFLECTION QUESTIONS:

1. What is a funny mistake you made, like my spaghetti sauce?

2. What event/situation in your life seemed like a mistake at the time but turned into a blessing?

BUILDING CHALLENGE

Thank God for choosing the cross for you, despite your mistakes.

---

[2] Jim Marshall, "Sometimes we're so ashamed of ourselves that we automatically feel like Jesus is too," Facebook, May 18. 2002, https://www.facebook.com/photo/?fbid=10221565289425128&set=gm.1704147366588342&idorvanity=1087956148207470.

PART TWO
Building

six

FOUNDATIONALLY BUILT

> **By the grace God has given me, I laid a foundation as a wise builder, and someone else is building on it. But each one should build with care.**
>
> 1 CORINTHIANS 3:10

THE FIRST STEP in building is also the most important part of a house: the foundation. I can guess that most of us don't think about this part of the home, unless it is shaken, has cracks, or was not built correctly in the first place. In your walk, there will be times when your faith is tested, when you learn how strong your foundation in God is. You may have to find ways to strengthen or reconfirm your commitment to God.

The foundation in current homes is almost always concrete, but the important thing is to build on something solid, like rock. We can describe certain people in our lives as being a rock. "People think of rocks as strong, solid, and unchanging. To call a person a rock means the same thing. That person is someone you can always rely on to help and support you."[1] God is referred to throughout the Bible as the rock of Israel and is the best example of reliability for us. Jesus is referred to as the cornerstone and the capstone, which are both important pieces in a building. The cornerstone is the one from which the foundation is built, whereas the capstone brings the whole building together at the top. Those words are interchangeable in Greek, but both apply to Jesus. "Jesus is the foundation of the church but also the capstone that holds everything together."[2] Or as it says in Colossians 1:17, "He is before all things, and in him all things hold together."

One of the most known Bible stories about building on the rock is in both the Gospels of Luke and Matthew.

> "As for everyone who comes to me and hears my words and puts them into practice, I will show you what they are like. They are like a man building a house, who dug

---

[1] "What Does You're My Rock Mean?" Writing Explained, accessed on November 5, 2023, https://writingexplained.org/idiom-dictionary/youre-my-rock.

[2] "What is the significance of a capstone in the Bible?" Got Questions, accessed on November 5, 2023, gotquestions.org/capstone-in-the-Bible.html.

down deep and laid the foundation on rock. When a flood came, the torrent struck that house but could not shake it, because it was well built. But the one who hears my words and does not put them into practice is like a man who built a house on the ground without a foundation. The moment the torrent struck that house, it collapsed and its destruction was complete."
–Luke 6:47–49 (see also Matthew 7:24–27)

To walk the walk is easier said than done. We are imperfect people; however, we can set our lives on the perfect foundation of God. "We walk the walk, not in perfection, but with dedication."[3] God chose Peter, an imperfect man, to lead. Jesus renamed Simon to Peter because the Greek name for Peter, Petros, means rock or stone. "'And I tell you that you are Peter, and on this rock I will build my church, and the gates of Hades will not overcome it'" (Matthew 16:18). Jesus knew Peter's foundation was built correctly, even though Peter made mistakes. Peter boldly rebuked Jesus at one point and then denied being a follower, after vehemently denying he would do that. And yet, Jesus could see past those moments. Or maybe those moments helped Peter seek God in a more vulnerable and open way. To know that he was shown mercy enabled him to be a better leader.

---

[3] Scott Schurle, beta reader comment, September 3, 2023.

In a group discussion about Peter's denial, one expressed their frustration that when tested, Peter failed. But what would have happened if Peter had said yes, he was a follower? Would he have been sentenced to death as well? We don't know for sure, but I would make that educated guess. How would the church have been built then? The other disciples, in turn, may have then run in fear. The church would still have been built because Christ is the foundation, but it probably would have looked different. Thankfully, God protected Peter and the other disciples, even when it appeared that they were disobedient in fleeing. Like in the Scripture about the foundation in a storm, Peter's faith was built on solid rock. Circumstances (storms) can try to shake it, yet our faith grows stronger through them. Storms show us that no matter what, God is with us and loves us. For me, knowing that has strengthened my faith. Other people may fall short, but God will never stop being our foundation, as long as we are willing to seek him.

It can be tempting to wonder why God protects some people, but doesn't protect others, or at least, it appears that way. I understand why people contrast Peter with Judas Iscariot, the man who betrayed Jesus. Judas Iscariot was also chosen as a disciple, and Jesus said it would have been better if he hadn't been born. But, like how Peter was protected by lying, Judas had a part in fulfilling prophecy and building the church. Hear me out. Judas heard the same sermons, saw the same miracles, and believed Jesus could be the Jewish people's interpretation of their Messiah, but he let worldly desires grow up through cracks in his foundation. Judas showed his cracks when he questioned about the woman who used oil on Jesus's feet instead of using the profits from selling the oil to give to the poor (John 12). It sounded like he was concerned about the poor, but it was about the money (worldly desires).

While Peter's faith became more solid, Judas let the cracks grow. After Jesus was arrested, Judas tried to return the money to the chief priests. He sought forgiveness from other people, but it doesn't say he sought God. Peter was redeemed when Jesus asked him, "Do you love me?" three times. Peter answered enthusiastically "yes" each time. I have heard he was asked three times because Peter denied Jesus three times. What we can learn from Peter is no matter what you have thought, said, or done, if you seek God, he still loves you and wants a relationship with you.

What can cause cracks in our foundation? In houses, the ground settling, natural disasters, and water leaks can all cause cracks. In our lives, a crack can be letting the circumstances around us dictate how strong our faith is. It can also mean how we let sinful thoughts turn into actions (cracks growing). Cracks form when we turn from God and towards the world. It is not uncommon to have some cracks in your foundation, but that is also because you are not perfect. This is when we repent and seek God's forgiveness.

What is one way to start building on the foundation of God, or maybe rebuild correctly? Baptism. Churches have differing views on when and how this occurs, but even Jesus was baptized at the start of his ministry. It is a statement of faith that we believe Jesus took on our sins once and for all. I was baptized as an infant, but I chose to recommit with an immersion baptism in January 2022. Before immersing me, Pastor Scott told me to "not fight him," which meant to not be resistant physically. But I can take that analogy to how we need to not be resistant to what God wants us to do and trust him. Once again, easier said than done. The only way I can describe my baptism is it was something between God and me. Not the pastor, not the other people in the congregation watching and clapping afterwards. It was just between God and me because I don't remember the actual immersion or several seconds afterwards. I remember "Don't fight me," and then walking up the steps out of the baptismal.

At first, I was upset that I didn't remember that moment of recommitment. But, with time, I believe God revealed to me that this was a private moment, so he had to block everything else out, even my own memory. It was for God's glory, not for me to gloat about. My faith has been tested since being re-baptized, but that commitment can't be taken from me. Even when there are temptations by evil spirits to not believe who I am in Christ, I have my foundation set in God.

When Jesus told the story about the builders, he didn't say there wouldn't be storms. On the contrary, storms are when our foundation is put to the test. But if you can keep your focus on God and have others in your life remind you of this, you can get through any storm. Even if it feels like some cracks have started in your foundation, could it be those cracks are there to let the light of Christ shine through?

REFLECTION QUESTIONS:
1. *How and when did you start following Christ?*
2. *How has a circumstance (storm) strengthened your foundation?*

BUILDING CHALLENGE

Make a recommitment to follow Christ through prayer, baptism, or write your recommitment on an index card to put up in your house. If you have never accepted Christ, my prayer is that you make that commitment today.

FIRM FOUNDATION
CODY CARNES

seven

GRACE-FILLED WOOD

You can think of homes and buildings like the game Jenga; when loads are unbalanced, structures fall down.[1]

ONCE THE FOUNDATION is set and you have all the plans in motion, it's time to start building up. This begins with the support beams, joists, and subflooring, most often using wood. This framework is what the rest of the house is built upon. Like the foundation, you may not understand the framework's importance. In our faith journey, we can overlook the importance of God's grace and mercy, especially if things are going well in our lives.

---

1 "What Is a Ceiling Joist?" Complete Building Solutions, accessed on December 10, 2023, https://cbsmn.com/ceiling-joist/.

When I was making the outline for this book, I asked my husband what the steps would be for building a house. One of the steps I had overlooked was this one. A joist is "a long thick piece of wood or metal that is used to support a floor or ceiling in a building."[2] The foundation was prepared for the floor joists with rods inserted in the concrete. Then, studded walls rise vertically from the floor to support the ceiling joists. Some of these walls are called load-bearing because if they aren't there, the house will collapse.

Then, the subflooring, usually made of plywood, is secured to the floor joists. It creates a level surface for the rest of the house to be built upon. These are the basics I have learned about this step that I never would've known if I hadn't written on this topic. I built my knowledge of house building through working on building my faith.

It can be easy to overlook or underappreciate God's sacrifice in showing us love through grace and mercy. We can hear words like grace and mercy and not know what they mean. They both involve kindness and compassion, but there is a difference between them. Mercy is "God's not punishing us as our sins deserve," and grace includes "bestowing a gift or favor.... In Scripture, mercy is often equated with a

---

2   Oxford Learner's Dictionary, s.v. "joist (n)," accessed December 22, 2023, https://www.oxfordlearnersdictionaries.com/us/definition/english/joist?q=joist.

deliverance from judgment...and grace is always the extending of a blessing to the unworthy."[3]

The first person in the Bible I thought of when I thought of a wooden framework was Noah. I can't imagine how much wood or the amount of time it took to build the ark to God's specifications. Noah's obedience in continuing to do what he was called to do was a testament to the strength of his foundation in God. Because of this obedience, God was willing to show Noah mercy. Noah was preparing for the storm that was coming, but I would take an educated guess that he also had to endure mocking and doubters while he built the ark. "Noah didn't stop building the ark to explain himself to every doubter and hater. Keep building and let the rain do the talking."[4]

It also would have been challenging to know that when the flood did come, all the creatures, except those he saved, would be wiped out. What we learn is that Noah was able to face the storm because he did it with God. Unlike Noah, we aren't told ahead of time what the storm will look like. That is a blessing because we may not choose to face those storms.

---

3   "What is the difference between mercy and grace?" Got Questions, accessed May 27, 2023, https://www.gotquestions.org/mercy-grace.html.

4   Lance Hucker, "Noah didn't stop building the ark to explain himself to very doubter and hater," Facebook, June 8, 2022, https://www.facebook.com/photo/?fbid=5259936744086876&set=a.285168758230391.

Noah stepped into the ark, but he had to wait for a sign for when he could step out. God gave Noah this sign of hope with the olive branch. "What's special about an olive leaf? An olive tree often resprouts even after it seems the tree has died."[5] The storms we face can feel like all hope is gone, but God is always with us. The key is to remain obedient and "Set your minds on things above, not on earthly things" (Colossians 3:2). Each storm will pass, and God reminds us of this promise in the rainbow.

Why did God call it an ark? The Hebrew word for ark means box or chest. Another meaning is that it is a form of protection, which gives comfort. In the story of Noah, when they entered the ark, God shut the door (Genesis 7:16). The story of Noah is one of many times God saved people. The story of Moses has many parallels. Moses was put in a basket, which can be translated to an ark, that was placed in the water to save his life.

> You can see the similarities between the ark that carried the remains of humanity that were worth saving along with the bare essentials to reestablish the animal kingdom, and the "ark" that carried Moses, who was to be a saviour figure—a prelude to the ultimate Messiah, both floating perilously off into the future. Both were

---

5   *NIV Quest Study Bible*, Grand Rapids, MI: Zondervan, 2011, p. 13.

absolutely critical for the future of humanity, and both carried great treasures.[6]

Once in the desert, what was Moses commanded to build? The *Ark* of the Covenant. What did it hold? The Ten Commandments, a jar of manna, and Aaron's staff that budded, which were reminders of God's covenant with His people.

In a literal sense, a covenant means a binding agreement, a legal contract. It is a seal between two or more parties. In a biblical sense, the word covenant derives from the same root word meaning "to cut." This means that in the culture of the Bible, covenant carried weight and was often cut, or sealed, with blood.[7]

Covenant, like grace and mercy, is another foundational piece of wood. God will show compassion by saving people from their sins and even blessing them beyond people's understanding.

If these stories are sounding a lot like Jesus's, it's no coincidence. My pastor has taught me to listen for echoes in

---

[6] "Why Is It Called an Ark?" One For Israel, accessed May 27, 2023, https://www.oneforisrael.org/bible-based-teaching-from-israel/why-is-it-called-an-ark/.

[7] Esther Kuhn, "What is a Covenant in the Bible?" Fellowship of Israel Related Ministries, November 5, 2020, https://firmisrael.org/learn/what-is-a-covenant-in-the-bible/.

Scripture, and there are a lot of them in these stories. Wood was needed for each project: Noah's Ark, the Ark of the Covenant, and ultimately, Jesus's cross. Each story is about saving people, a few at first with Noah, the Israelites from Egypt, and ultimately, all people who believe in Jesus's sacrifice. Jesus said he didn't come to get rid of the old covenant, but to fulfill it. Jesus took on the load of all our sins as a gift of both grace and mercy. Like the olive branch, Jesus gave us hope in eternal life through his resurrection and extending that blessing (grace) to us as well. "For God so loved the world that he gave his one and only Son, that whoever believes in him shall not perish but have eternal life" (John 3:16).

I realize this chapter may feel heavy or deep (yes, I meant to make comparisons to heavy wood and deep water). My personal connection is a lighter one. My husband and I were watching *The Big Bang Theory,* and the characters were trying to determine whether a wall was load-bearing or not in preparation for a renovation. They went under the house, and my husband pointed out, "That's not how you would make that determination." In the many times I had watched that episode, it never dawned on me that they would have needed to look up in the attic instead. So, instead of looking down around at earthly things, look up!

GRACE-FILLED WOOD ✝ 51

REFLECTION QUESTIONS:
1. When was there a time that you felt you deserved punishment, but you received mercy instead?
2. Why are both grace and mercy vital to building faith?

BUILDING CHALLENGE

Go outside, look up to the sky, and thank God for his grace and mercy through Christ.

BUILD A BOAT
COLTON DIXON

eight

FRAMEWORK OF PRAYER

I have so much to do that I shall spend the first three hours in prayer.

MARTIN LUTHER[1]

ONCE YOU HAVE all of the joists and the load-bearing walls set in place, it is time to finish the framing of the house. Framing out each room and making the openings for windows and doors fills out the skeleton of the house. In a similar way, our relationship with God, who is our foundation, needs to include a framework of prayer. Prayer is how we build our relationship with God.

---

1   Martin Luther, "I have so much to do that I shall spend the first three hours in prayer," AZ Quotes, accessed on December 23, 2023, https://www.azquotes.com/quote/353476.

The first person in the Bible that came to my mind when I thought of walls was Nehemiah. He led the remnant of Israel to rebuild the walls around Jerusalem. When Nehemiah first heard about the condition of Jerusalem, he wept, fasted, and, most importantly, prayed. Prayer is the backbone that supports all our plans. Have you tried to pursue something without praying about it first? Doesn't usually work out too well, does it? We tend to think it's our own power and strength making things happen and don't rely on God as we should.

Nehemiah prayed first, and then he began the rebuilding process. But first, let me explain the backstory. The Jewish people living in Judah, including the city of Jerusalem, were conquered by the Babylonians and taken into captivity. Jerusalem's wall and the Jewish temple were destroyed. Then, the Persian Empire conquered the Babylonians and allowed the Jewish people to return to Jerusalem. The Jewish people rebuilt the temple, though not as elaborate as the original, but they hadn't rebuilt the wall. Why was that important? As Nehemiah told the Jewish people, "You see the trouble we are in: Jerusalem lies in ruins, and its gates have been burned with fire. Come, let us rebuild the wall of Jerusalem, and we will no longer be in disgrace" (Nehemiah 2:17). This meant they would then be seen as having a strong God that is pleased with them.

The wall also provided physical protection. The wall was approximately forty feet high and eight feet thick and looped for over two miles around the city. Nehemiah was able to lead multiple groups in the rebuilding process, which must have taken a lot of planning. Unfortunately, it also came with opposition, mocking, and negativity. What impresses me is Nehemiah rallied the people on this project, and they completed it in just fifty-two days. But then again, he prayed and planned for four months beforehand, and "'with God, all things are possible'" (Matthew 19:26).

We are called to pray in all situations. One of the results of prayer is that God will guide us to face both the good and bad in each situation. When I looked through a Bible study I had done on Nehemiah, I found a question that asked, "What do you long to see God bring full circle in your life? Write it down even if you've given up hope or think it impossible."[2] I did this study in 2015 and wrote "writing my story," which meant writing about my faith. I didn't start writing my first book until four years later. I had felt the calling to write for many years and had even tried a few other times to write. But God needed to prepare me more.

In the actual process of writing and publishing my first book, I was challenged to live out those lessons and be sifted, or as a quote I had found said, "Your calling is going to crush you.... Your calling will come with cups, thorns, and sifting

---

[2] Kelly Minter, *Nehemiah: A Heart That Can Break*, Nashville, TN: LifeWay Press, 2017, p. 150.

that are necessary for your mantle to be authentic, humble and powerful. Your crushing won't be easy, because your assignment is not easy."[3] What that means is I had to work on the areas I didn't feel were good enough to be chosen for this assignment. Thankfully, God has shown me over and over since I started writing that he was and always will be with me. Also, like Nehemiah, I have people who are there to support me in all areas of my life.

Nehemiah can be an inspiration to anyone wanting to pursue their calling. This doesn't mean the road is all peaches and cream or that you won't feel like you're hitting your own walls when walking out your faith. "I told my friend that I'm emotionally 'hitting a wall' and she said 'Sometimes walls are there so we can lean on them and rest.'"[4] Prayer can help us find hope when something feels overwhelming.

Another part of building walls is framing out the doors and windows. One way to look at this is: how much are you willing to share about yourself with others? You have to open the door to let people see who you truly are. While it is important to have walls (a.k.a. boundaries) with other

---

[3] A Closer Look, "Your Calling Is Going to Crush You," Facebook, November 20, 2021, https://www.facebook.com/closerlookbible/photos/a.1100719456971702/1513634065680237.

[4] I've got something positive to say, "I've told my friend I'm emotionally," Facebook, March 4, 2021, https://www.facebook.com/IveGotSomething-PositiveToSay/photos/a.2436669939711848/3858066490905512/)

people, it is equally important to let your authentic self out. That vulnerability is a testament to showing love to God, others, and yourself. It doesn't mean that you won't feel rejection or negativity when you open up. But remember, as a man, Jesus experienced extreme rejection from people around him. He went away and prayed time and time again to build his relationship with his Father and gain strength. Thankfully, Jesus showed his authentic self and paid the highest price for all of us, which only he could do: he died for our salvation.

One thing you hear people comment on when searching for a home on house hunting shows is how much natural light they observe in the home. A lot of windows can brighten up a room. That can be true about our own lives too. A job, hobbies, and activities that give you joy will brighten your life. That joy, in turn, can shine more light onto others.

There are also experiences that bring out darker moments. One of our dogs, Pasha, was losing her eyesight, which seemed to happen overnight. She seemed to be okay most of the time during the day but would get disoriented at night. We had to be right there with her so she wouldn't run into walls, fall down the steps, or be stuck out in the dark alone. Having times of darkness helps you appreciate the light more. Both light and dark experiences build your faith, but in different ways. The lesson is to seek the light of Christ to guide you. One of those ways is through prayer.

Let us use the examples of both Nehemiah and Jesus and seek God through prayer for everything. The time we spend in prayer is not wasted. God is able to build us in ways that only he can. While things can be costly when you open up and show vulnerability, it is even more costly to do it without God.

REFLECTION QUESTIONS:
1. What project that seemed impossible have you completed with God's help?
2. What experience of darkness helped you appreciate the light? (It's okay to be vulnerable when sharing.)

BUILDING CHALLENGE

Pray for strength to pursue God's calling in your life. If you haven't identified your calling, that's a great place to start the prayer.

TRUTH BE TOLD

MATTHEW WEST

nine

ROOF OF TRUST AND PROTECTION

> "Have I not commanded you? Be strong and courageous. Do not be afraid; do not be discouraged, for the Lord your God will be with you wherever you go."
>
> JOSHUA 1:9

The next step is putting on the trusses, sheathing, and the roof. "Sheathing is the supporting structure that acts as a cover for the surfaces of a building. The main function of sheathing is to provide a surface where other materials can be applied to ... It also provides additional structural integrity to buildings."[1] There are many types of roofing to choose from, depending on the

---

1   "What is OSB Sheathing used for?" Silvaris, May 4, 2021, https://www.silvaris.com/what-is-osb-sheathing-used-for/.

pitch (steepness). Getting up to the roof can require steps of trust while climbing up a ladder. Likewise, part of building your faith is putting trust in God, even when you feel uncertain about how things will turn out.

Each part of this building phase requires trusting the team you are working with. The trusses have to be lifted up to be set on the framing of the house. It can be a more daunting task on a multi-level house because the heights are riskier for the installers. Sometimes all *we* can do is trust in God that everything will be okay. We may not see or know how he protects us in those moments, but he doesn't stop loving us.

When I searched the word "roof" in my Bible app, two stories came up that illustrated trust. The first was Rahab hiding spies on her flat roof. Who were these spies, and why did they need to hide? Joshua had succeeded Moses as leader of the Israelites as they were about to enter the Promised Land. He sent two spies to scope out the land, including Jericho. They were seen entering the house of Rahab, who was described as a prostitute. In my Bible commentary, it states they may have chosen that house because "It was no doubt a good place to find out information and blend in with other travelers with no questions asked."[2]

However, they didn't blend in enough. Fortunately, Rahab chose to hide the spies and then lied to the king of Jericho that

---

2   *NIV Quest Study Bible*, Grand Rapids, MI: Zondervan, 2011, p. 309.

they had already left. The spies trusted Rahab, a stranger. This is where God showed his protection and love for both parties. In return for hiding the spies, Rahab asked for her family to be protected when the Israelites took the city. She hung a scarlet cord outside her window, and the spies honored her request. I believe God led the spies to her house because he wanted Rahab's family to be part of his family. As we trust the sheathing and the roof to protect us from weather, we can trust God's love for us, even when our circumstances may not appear to be fair or we don't understand why they occur.

This story made me wonder: how was it possible to hide someone on a roof? "She [Rahab] had taken them up to the roof and hidden them under the stalks of flax she had laid out on the roof" (Joshua 2:6). Flax was a common plant in that area, and the people used their roofs as a place to dry them. Flax was "used in forming articles of clothing such as girdles, also cords and bands."[3] Linen is made out of flax. In my Bible dictionary under "plants of flax/source of linen" was the Scripture about the burial of Jesus: "Going to Pilate, he [Joseph of Arimathea] asked for Jesus's body. Then he took it down, wrapped it in linen cloth and placed it in a tomb cut in the rock, one in which no one had yet been laid" (Luke 23: 52–53). Joseph of Arimathea showed his love for Jesus as

---

3   Bible Study Tools, Thomas Nelson, s.v. "flax (n.)," accessed on November 5, 2023, https://www.biblestudytools.com/dictionary/flax/.

Joseph tried to observe Jewish law by assisting in Jesus's burial. Rahab covered the spies with flax to save them. Generations later, flax was used to cover Jesus's body as he covered all our sins.

Another story is about the man who was lowered through the roof to seek Jesus's healing. So many people had gathered to hear Jesus, there was no way for a paralyzed man to reach him. His friends took him to the roof, made an opening, and lowered him with some sort of ropes. During this time, access to the roof was via stairway because they used their roofs for more than just coverings. It could be for sleeping or, as in Rahab's case, putting crops out to dry. Because of its regular use, when they made an opening, it wasn't like pulling shingles and cutting through plywood.

> The roof itself was flat and made of tile sandwiched around brush or branch insulation. To lift a section of the roof, then dig through the insulation and remove a tile from the ceiling was not a drastic measure.[4]

Even if it may not sound as impressive, the men were determined to get their friend to Jesus because they cared about their friend and trusted he would be healed. The paralyzed man trusted and put his faith in his friends to get him there. These two stories show us that if we trust God, he will

---

4   *NIV Quest Study Bible*, Grand Rapids, MI: Zondervan, 2011, p. 1478.

put the right people in our lives to help us. We need to be willing to accept help from others, which, for many of us, may mean learning how to receive that help.

The first thing I have to face when I want to help install a roof is the fear of getting up on the roof. I don't have a fear of heights, but falling from them is another story. Once I get up and away from the edge, I am okay. For me, the other scary part is getting onto the ladder to get back down. I have to trust that the ladder will stay still and I can get myself in the right position to get off the roof. While on the roof, I do well getting supplies where they are needed. I have learned how to cut the shingles to finish the row, and my husband and I get into a good working rhythm.

When we redid the roof of our house several years ago, we had to tear off the old layers. Yes, layers. Usually, you only have a maximum of two. But somehow, the old part of our house had at least three, possibly four. That was a painstakingly slow process of peeling back to get to the plywood. Sometimes in our faith walk, we have to reassess what our trust level is. It may take a reset of trust through forgiveness and letting go of the past. Thankfully, we can always trust that God wants the best for us. Our circumstances may have us shaking on a ladder, but we build our faith in each step up. Taking steps up the trust ladder can feel scary with other people, but we can be reassured that God will be with us.

REFLECTION QUESTIONS:
1. *Who in your life would you trust to lower you from a roof to help you?*
2. *What area in your life can you find a way to take a step toward trusting God, others, or yourself?*

BUILDING CHALLENGE

Thank one of the people in your life who has gone out of their way to show they cared about you.

ten

WIRED IN LOVING YOURSELF

Do not conform to the pattern of this world, but be transformed by the renewing of your mind. Then you will be able to test and approve what God's will is—his good, pleasing and perfect will.

ROMANS 12:2

ONCE THE WALLS are up, all the wiring, duct work, and plumbing can be installed. It is important to have these steps done correctly so the house can operate properly. Our bodies, including our minds, are like a house. It may require rewiring to function in a healthier way. This work is challenging, but it is an act of loving yourself.

It is important to have all the wiring, duct work, and plumbing installed correctly. If not, it can cause destruction, like a fire or flooded rooms. The clean-up process can be a feat in and of itself. This can be applied to the human body as well. We don't think about how amazing the brain works, which is the most complex wiring. We only appreciate all of it working when something goes wrong, like an injury or a painful experience. Then, it requires our desire to get back to homeostasis or, even better, come back stronger.

Instead of using a biblical story in this chapter, I'll use a story from a TV show. I was rewatching *Dawson's Creek*, a show from the 1990s, and an interaction between two characters got my attention. It was a conversation between Pacey and Andie, a couple who had broken up, but Andie wanted to reconcile.

> PACEY: "Sometimes it's harder to rebuild something than it is to start from scratch."
>
> ANDIE: "Why?"
>
> PACEY: "That picture you have in your mind of the way something was, it's never going to be that way again."
>
> ANDIE: "Yeah, but it could be better."
>
> PACEY: "Yeah, it could be, depending on how badly damaged it was in the first place."
>
> ANDIE: "How badly damaged was it?"
>
> PACEY: "It was pretty much totaled."[1]

---

1 Gregory Prange, dir. *Dawson's Creek*, Season 3, episode 6, "Secrets and Lies," aired November 10, 1999, viewed via compact disc.

It was impactful to me because I could understand Pacey's hesitation to rebuild after a painful experience. Rebuilding depends on how badly damaged a person or relationship is in the first place. You may not know what has been rewired differently until you open the walls and inspect everything thoroughly. I mentioned my depression and anxiety in a previous chapter, but I needed to explore deeper causes that made my mental health struggles more intense. I have always felt the need to people-please and had the mindset of needing to earn people's love for me. This led me to take on more and more at church to the point of complete burnout and compassion fatigue. I was so exhausted, but I felt like I couldn't give it up. I was so scared that people only cared about me for what I was doing, not for who I was.

Even though I was afraid, I gave up many of my commitments at church. That was one of the hardest things I have ever done; it shattered my heart. I didn't know if I could rebuild my relationship with that church. As Pacey said, I knew it was never going to be the same. But something deep inside me, a love for myself, took priority. I hope those of you who have this same people-pleasing mindset can acknowledge that loving yourself is okay, and it's okay to put your own needs first sometimes. We can all be more diligent in how we take care of ourselves, like Jesus said, "Love your neighbor as yourself" (Matthew 22:39). We are called to love others, but it also includes loving ourselves.

As I started the process of inspecting my wiring, I knew I needed to have my brain physically inspected. I was concerned that my history of seizures and depression could have altered how my neurons communicated. I was also having trouble with my memory at times. Both an EEG and brain MRI were ordered. My MRI came back as "unremarkable," which meant it was normal, but I wish they had a better word than unremarkable. It is quite remarkable that God was able to create our bodies. I was thankful that nothing permanent was altered.

Another approach I used was going to therapy. A couple of months after giving up my main commitments at church, I began a more intensive form of therapy. It was called Brain Synchronization Therapy (BST), which is similar to Eye Movement Desensitization and Reprocessing (EMDR). I remember learning about it in one of my psychology classes in college, but the experience itself is its own beast. My therapist described BST as being gentler than EMDR, but every session I did was as exhausting as an intense workout in the gym. BST replicates the eye movements that occur when you sleep, which is why it can be tiring and draining.

I learned that my brain's wiring wasn't processing negative emotions, so I was holding onto them instead of letting them go. In this process, BST helped me to identify my core fears and insecurities, which were all connected to these negative memories. BST allowed me to feel those negative emotions again in a safe environment. It then let my brain pack those memories away properly. Consequently, when I recall a particular memory, it doesn't upset me all over again. How they figured out how to help me reprogram my brain is a miracle in itself.

Unfortunately, or fortunately, during this rewiring, it brought out other negative memories, ones I hadn't thought of in years. My therapist said if you allow yourself to feel whatever emotion that comes up by acknowledging it, you can then release it. Allowing yourself to feel the sadness or anger instead of ruminating is a type of reprogramming. It's like flipping the switch once the wiring is set. I just didn't know the switch was malfunctioning until it started working properly.

Another way someone described this process was that it was like cleaning out a hoarder's house. Think of all the junk and boxes you would have to go through to see what was salvageable or not. You start clearing out boxes in one room, which gives you confidence that you can do it. But then, you turn and look at the next room of junk, which makes your heart sink. The rewiring I did was just as challenging to sort through, and I couldn't rush the process. But once I started, I became more determined to finish.

It came as no surprise to me that, as I was working on this chapter, the movie *Inside Out* came on TV one evening. The movie is about all the different emotions we experience, including Joy, Sadness, Anger, Disgust, and Fear. The movie did a great job showing that all emotions are okay to have. It's often through difficult times that we build relationships and our faith. While we would all like to stay in Joy, there are many memories that bring a mixture of emotions. One of the main lessons of the film was that while it is important to have Joy, "They [Friends] came to help because of Sadness."[2] Part of recovering from burnout is giving up the idea that I failed somehow. This is where I needed to show love to myself by forgiving myself. "You don't have to like what happened. Simply let go of the illusion that it could have been any different."[3] This is not a quick or easy process, but if you can trust God in the process, it does help to build your faith.

The process is, well, a process. Just because the actual rewiring work may be done, that doesn't mean there will not be setbacks. Fortunately, even though they can be frustrating, they can be opportunities to see how much progress you've made. The process of rewiring my brain helped me to appreciate healthy functioning in all aspects: physical, mental, and spiritual. It may require work to rewire, but God is with us on this rebuilding project. Take on the challenge to show love for yourself in any way God shows you.

---

[2] Pete Docter and Ronnie Del Carmen, dir. *Inside Out*, Pixar, 2015, viewed via DirecTV.

[3] The Soul Journey with Sarah Moussa, "A Forgiving Moment," Facebook, August 27, 2022, https://www.facebook.com/permalink.php?story_fbid=pfbid0iLjpw7MMNvJn32PXAX-RHg1eGLWUQ148Uhcbzohx5mKmtEniN7EmckRi6GqwLu-FAUl&id=100069505335894.

REFLECTION QUESTIONS:
1. *What area in your life or relationship did you choose to rebuild, despite the challenge of it?*
2. *How does feeling all your emotions help build your faith?*

BUILDING CHALLENGE

Do one act of self-love today. And remember to continue them.

eleven

INSULATING OURSELVES WITH SCRIPTURE

> **Love is patient, love is kind. It does not envy, it does not boast, it is not proud. It does not dishonor others, it is not self-seeking, it is not easily angered, it keeps no record of wrongs. Love does not delight in evil but rejoices with the truth. It always protects, always trusts, always hopes, always perseveres.**
>
> 1 CORINTHIANS 13:4-7

ONCE ALL THE wiring and plumbing are set in the walls, it's time for insulation and sheetrock. This will seal the inside part of the house, protecting it from the outside world. To help build our faith, we need to be insulated with words of Scripture. Like walls protect us from hot and cold weather and outside noise, the words of Scripture can defend our hearts and minds against negativity and evil spirits that try to invade us.

In today's world, it is so easy to access Scripture, but do we go the next step and memorize it in our hearts? I picked part of what is known to be the "love chapter" in Corinthians as my opening Scripture, but how many can say they have it memorized? I will be the first to admit I don't. Love is something we are called to do; it's not just a feeling. We may not feel like applying the "love is patient" piece to situations in which we are impatient, but it's what God wants us to do. That is the difference between just memorizing a verse and actually knowing Scripture. My pastor pointed out to me that the Pharisees had memorized Scripture, but asked if they really knew it. My answer would be "no" because they would quote Scripture and hold other people to impossible standards, but not apply it to themselves. Faith building includes not just reading Scripture, but actively doing the things we say we believe. We all fall short, but we need to keep trying.

Many people during Jesus's time did not have access to the scrolls or could not read. They had to repeat it over and over so it could not only sink into their minds, but also into their hearts. That is probably why Ezra found it so important to read the hidden scrolls they found in the temple. We all need that repetition to strengthen ourselves in God.

Memorizing Scripture is very useful when we are tested. Jesus provides the best example of this when he was in the desert. He had fasted for forty days and forty nights, and then "the tempter" (Satan) came to him. Satan offered him three temptations: turn stones into bread, throw himself down from the highest point of the temple, and bow down and worship Satan in exchange for the world. Each time, Jesus responded with Scripture from what we know as Deuteronomy in the Old Testament. Satan knew Jesus's power and tried to steer him away from his calling. We can also be steered away from serving God by believing the lies the tempter tries on us.

One of the ways Satan tries to tempt us is by using Scripture out of context. We all know the story of Eve and Adam being tempted in the garden. The snake (devil) twisted what God said about not eating from the Tree of Knowledge. Eve fell for the lie, then Adam, which caused them to be separated from God as it brought sin into the world. But the devil also used Scripture with Jesus in the desert. I have heard the Scripture about Jesus being tempted in the desert read many times in church during Lent, but as I read along this past year, something new stuck out. In the second temptation, the devil said, "For it is written: 'He will command his angels concerning you, and they will lift you up in their hands, so that you will not strike your foot against a stone'" (Matthew 4:6). What caught my attention was the reference to Psalm 91. In one of my conversations with my pastor, he suggested that I read a prayer of protection, such as Psalm 91, when I am struggling with the negative thoughts that come with depression and anxiety. I have read that prayer many times, and it calms my mind enough to give me strength to fight. The irony is what the devil intended to use for harm, God turns around for good. But I had to remember to go read it since I didn't have it memorized. That's okay because the victory was remembering it and then using it.

Learning how to insulate your mind with the words of Scripture takes time and effort. A Bible study I recently completed was called *Truth Filled* by Ruth Chou Simons. In it, she guides you to preaching the good news to yourself. "To grow and be 'built up,' then, is a result of being nourished through the Word of God."[1] It is something that doesn't happen overnight. As in putting a house together, it happens piece by piece. Our faith builds in the same way, and the more we have to protect our minds, the stronger we will be able to resist the negative forces.

My first job as a hostess in a restaurant provides an example of the importance of memorization. Two of the main tasks of the job were seating guests and taking carry-out orders. I had to memorize table numbers to seat guests in different sections, which seemed like it would be relatively easy to learn. The more complicated part of the job was taking an order over the phone. It was a barbeque restaurant, so there were

---

[1] Ruth Chou Simons, *Truthfilled: The Practice of Preaching to Yourself Through Every Season*, Nashville, TN: LifeWay Press, 2021, p. 77.

a lot of options for each order. There was also a computer system to navigate. It was overwhelming. I wanted to be an expert at all the tasks right away, but it took time to get the hang of it. Or, in my case, it "wasn't working," and they let me go after only a short time. I learned not to be discouraged by a task that takes longer to master, like memorizing, and to be patient with myself as we all learn at different speeds.

It's in the trials and errors in life where we grow confident in our skills. My next job was at a college bookstore, which was a better fit for me. With each job I have had since, I have been challenged to learn new skills and build upon the ones I had. It can be the same in our faith journey. We find where our gifts and talents can be best used, but we have to be willing to keep pursuing them. This is a lifelong process, and each experience builds us to the next one.

The important lesson is to keep adding the words of Scripture to your heart every chance you can. Using memorized Scripture is a great way to pray, especially when you don't know what else to say. Let the words of Scripture protect you and help you confidently face the storm with God.

REFLECTION QUESTIONS:

1. *How have the words of Scripture been a form of protection and comfort for you?*
2. *Read Psalm 91. What stands out to you?*

BUILDING CHALLENGE

Memorize a verse or two of Scripture.

twelve

SOLID WALL OF BELIEVERS

Therefore encourage one another and build each other up, just as in fact you are doing.

1 THESSALONIANS 5:11

Now it's time to get the outside walls completed. There are many choices, including siding, stucco, brick, or log cabin. Like in "The Three Little Pigs," you want to make sure your house is built with something sturdy so that it can't easily fall. One way is to find a community of believers in which you can build your faith.

One of the sturdiest buildings is built with logs. I recently had the opportunity to take a tour of a lodge in which all the walls were built with logs on a remote hillside built forty years ago. The amount of precision and time, not to mention the heavy logs, was admirable. Each log had to be placed one by one, and plans had to accommodate this type of wall structure.

For example, the light switches were horizontal. As I walked around, I felt the security and stability within those walls. Like the sturdy logs, having a strong group of believers to support one another is crucial.

> And let us consider how we may spur one another on toward love and good deeds, not giving up meeting together, as some are in the habit of doing, but encouraging one another—and all the more as you see the Day approaching. –Hebrews 10: 24–25

It can be challenging to build up the church when there are hurt feelings or offenses. We can even take it to the point of not wanting to be a part of a church community because of it. One area of love that builds our faith is forgiving others. It may be forgiving someone in your family, a friend, a stranger, or someone in your church community. It's right in the prayer that Jesus taught us, "'forgive us our debts, as we also have forgiven our debtors'" (Matthew 6:12). God forgives our sins, but we are commanded to extend that same forgiveness to others. To forgive someone is both easy and hard. It can be hard to let go of the hurt. My therapist had told me once that even if the intent wasn't to be hurtful, in words or actions, the impact was still there. Like when we have a physical injury, we didn't intend to get hurt, but we still have healing to do. Jesus showed us the importance of forgiveness when he forgave those who crucified him. While on the cross, he said, "Father, forgive them, for they do not know what they are doing" (Luke 23:34). If he could forgive them, then we can find a way to forgive others as well.

When I decided to give up the worship team, I had a lot of built-up anger, hurt, resentment, and unforgiveness towards others. I had been so focused on making sure everyone else enjoyed the service that I lost focus on the purpose: to worship God. It was like the story of Martha and Mary. I was being Martha, task-oriented, when I should have taken more time to sit at Jesus's feet like Mary. In conversations with different pastors recently, many shared they also can struggle with focus during a worship service. I am thankful that God showed me that I wasn't alone in this area.

Losing focus in worship and unforgiveness was affecting my relationship with God. These types of challenges can include anything that is coming between you and God, and we are called to lay those things at the foot of the cross. Jesus describes what to do when you are angry with someone else: "Therefore, if you are offering your gift at the altar and there remember that your brother or sister has something against you, leave your gift there in front of the altar. First go and be reconciled to them; then come and offer your gift" (Matthew 5:23–24). I didn't understand that verse until I was faced with unresolved anger and unforgiveness. But in God's loving way, he helped me confess my loss of focus by reminding me about the heart of worship through a song called "The Heart of Worship" by Matt Redman.

Once I was able to confess my loss of focus and unforgiveness, I was able to start the process of forgiving others and myself for things that had happened. Forgiveness includes letting go of the past. It also may mean stepping away from the people or place that hurt you, and that's ok. It may be part of God's plan to heal your heart. Forgiveness does not have to include an apology from the other person, but it does take our willingness to let go of the pain. I have found that my relationships became sturdier as I forgave.

Why is forgiving others a part of building up the Church? The apostles and first believers saw their communities as their "ekklesia," the Greek translation of church or gathering. "We're to be assemblies of God's authorized people who bring the good news, peace, and justice of God to the places that we live."[1] I like that description of how we should be viewing church. If you look at the letters that Paul wrote to the different emerging Christian communities, there was discord and strife. He instructs them to keep unified in Christ. Unfortunately, the more time has passed since Jesus's time, the more division and splintering of that solid wall has occurred. I can only imagine how this infighting breaks God's heart, seeing all the hatred over love.

Forgiveness expands into another one of Jesus's commands: "You have heard that it was said, 'Love your neighbor and hate

---

[1] Mark D. Roberts, Life for Leaders email, May 21, 2022.

your enemy.' But I tell you, love your enemies and pray for those who persecute you, that you may be children of your Father in heaven" (Matthew 5:43–45). Jesus continues his sermon to say we can love the people who care about us too, but he challenges us to extend that love to people who may not care about us.

It's hard to think about having enemies in our lives, but they can be people who have different beliefs than us, including political or religious. It can be tempting to bash the other side, but instead, we are called to love. "Be merciful to those who doubt; save others by snatching them from the fire; to others show mercy mixed with fear—hating even the clothing stained by corrupted flesh" (Jude 22–23). "According to this, our evangelism should be characterized by mercy for the sinner and a healthy hatred of sin and its effect."[2] As we build our Christian walls, let us not build only around ourselves. As Christians, we have to remember that people are watching our words and actions. We also need to show that it is ok to extend grace, which also means asking for forgiveness when we have hurt someone.

One of the biggest lessons I have learned was how important it is to have a group of believers supporting and caring for

---

[2] "Are we to love the sinner but hate the sin?" God Questions, accessed on December 30, 2023, https://www.gotquestions.org/love-sinner-hate-sin.html.

you. That ideal is in a church community, but I understand it may not be for everyone. It's important to be in the pews to build your faith and fill up with God's Word. We need to then get out of the pews to help build others' faith. "A follower of Jesus Christ is not called to sit in a pew. A follower of Jesus Christ is called to share the Good News with each and every person they meet."[3] Let the walls you focus on building be ones that build up the community of believers!

REFLECTION QUESTIONS:
1. How are you building your community of believers?
2. Who do you need to forgive or seek forgiveness from?

BUILDING CHALLENGE

Pray for a group of people that you may see as your imagined enemy.

THE HEART OF WORSHIP
MATT REDMAN

---

3   Scott Schurle, Central Christian Church, sermon, Pueblo, CO, May 21, 2023, accessed online July 1, 2023, https://www.youtube.com/watch?v=sfo_fV4Si5k.

thirteen

COLORFUL SUFFERING

The Lord has told you what is good, and this what he requires of you: to do what is right, to love mercy, and to walk humbly with your God.

MICAH 6:8, CEV

ONCE YOU HAVE sheetrock up, it's time to finish the walls. You start by sealing the seams with tape, then finish with texture and paint. The paint colors are the first real personal touch people will notice: neutral versus bright, mellow versus wild. Do you see God as being neutral or brightly shining through situations?

Before painting, you must first tape to seal the seams between sheetrock pieces. Then texturing is applied to the walls to give some character. That is one thing you hear a lot of comments about on house hunting shows: people looking for a home that has character. Several years ago, we went looking at new homes to get ideas for our own house. We noticed that a few had skipped the texture part and went straight to the painting. Covering up the seams is not our ultimate goal. Instead, the goal is finding restoration, healing, a feeling of wholeness. This process includes healing from a physical or mental wound. As you heal, scars are often left behind, but those wounds help to shape and build your testimony and unique character and draw you closer to God.

After taping and texturing comes the painting. I can barely draw a stick figure, but I can slap some paint on a wall. I'm a little messy and not the best painter, but it does give me joy. When I moved into my husband's house, he had one color: white. He said white covers up any imperfections, and I couldn't argue with that point. But I did add some color to his life, in a couple of the rooms at least. The house I helped paint in Greensburg, Kansas, on a mission trip was what we called "barn red." The choice of red was a bold statement as it brought more attention, and you could see any imperfections more clearly.

What do the choices of paint color have to do with our faith? It is how we paint ourselves, one another, our situations, and God in our interpretation of suffering. Do we view our suffering as a form of punishment for sinning (blood red) or think we shouldn't suffer because we are white as snow? The book of Job addresses this question of suffering. Job was described as "blameless and upright; he feared God and shunned evil" (Job 1:1). God gave Satan permission to afflict

Job with any form of suffering he chose, except to take his life. Job lost all his livestock, all his children, and was inflicted with a painful skin condition. His wife and his friends questioned why he wouldn't curse God. Job is described as the prime example of patience and loyalty to God. That doesn't mean he didn't wrestle with why all this suffering was happening. Even though Job didn't curse (blame) God, he brought his complaints to God. "I would state my case before him and fill my words with arguments" (Job 23:4). God responded by asking Job if he was there during the creation, had control over the weather or animals, and so on (see Job chapters 38–41).

While it can be tempting to question why something is happening in your life, that it doesn't seem fair, we have to remember that we don't have the full picture. This is where our faith is tested and we are challenged to trust in God even if, or especially when, relief doesn't come quickly. You may question how much suffering you can endure, like when someone tells you that God won't give you more than you can handle. Angie Smith addresses this misconception about being tempted/suffering in her book *Chasing God* by first quoting Scripture.

> God is faithful, who will not allow you to be tempted beyond what you are able, but with the temptation will provide a way of escape also, so that you will be able to endure it (1 Corinthians 10:13). It's not talking about

what you can 'handle.' Because quite frankly, everything in life is more than you can "handle." Which is why you need Him.[1]

The point is that we need to seek God at all times and in every situation.

Job is one of a few examples in the Bible where he asks God to put him out of his misery. Elijah did the same thing after defeating the Baal priests and running for his life. Both begged for death to come swiftly, but it wasn't their time. Jesus even prayed earnestly in the garden of Gethsemane for the cup to be removed from him, if it was God's will. Jesus knew what suffering he was about to endure, and that had to be an overwhelming feeling. Along with the physical pain, he knew his disciples would abandon him. What gives me comfort in these examples is God didn't punish or condemn them for crying out. Instead, God gave them comfort and the strength to endure any and all suffering that was to come.

I know how it feels to want so badly for the pain and suffering to end. I was tempted to take my own life on two occasions in 2022. Even though I had people who cared about me in my life, I struggled to believe that was true. I felt completely alone and hopeless. The only explanation I have for how I

---

[1] Angie Smith, *Chasing God*, Nashville, TN: B & H Publishing Group, 2014, p. 128–9.

made it through those times was that I did what I could to seek God, and he showed me mercy. I then wondered if I was still worthy of God's love because I saw the red paint splattered all over me. It reminded me of a promise I made while on a retreat as a teenager. "As I was sitting looking outside into the darkness, I saw a light from a light post shining directly to me. I felt it was God communicating to me, saying, 'You shouldn't think about committing suicide. There are too many people out there in the world who care about you.'"[2] The guilt, the red paint, I felt was because I almost broke my promise to God that I made that night as a teenager.

The first time, the suicidal thoughts lessened after a few hours. The second time, I couldn't get the thoughts out of my head. I decided to check myself into a facility for a few days for my own safety. By doing so, I showed myself that I was willing to keep trying. A couple of weeks after leaving the facility, I got a text from one of the people I had met there, asking for the suicide prevention hotline. For the next few hours, I prayed fervently for protection, but also felt truly thankful for the first time. I went from feeling shame and guilt to thanking God for protecting me. That was the beginning of feeling God's forgiveness. That red paint had disappeared, covered white as snow. God remembered my sinful thoughts no more, but I had to receive that forgiveness. Even though it didn't feel like I was

---

2   Rebecca Nolting, journal entry, May 25, 1996.

being very faithful during those moments, I can see now I was doing my best. God was there to protect me from myself. It is in the dark times that you appreciate times of joy even more.

The good news is God isn't neutral in wanting to be a part of comforting us when we are suffering. He can tape up our wounds with love, texture our mess into a message, and paint over all our sins through Christ. Let's use these times of struggle, suffering, pain, and weakness as a way to rely on God more. This will undoubtedly build your faith for what else may come.

Advice that I received when I was battling suicidal thoughts was that praying to God could only go so far. Seek the help you need because even if you don't feel like anyone cares, God loves you, and you matter!

REFLECTION QUESTIONS:
1. *How do you view suffering and struggles?*
2. *What pain or struggle brought you closer to God?*

BUILDING CHALLENGE

Reach out to a person in your life that struggles with mental health. It can be as simple as telling them you love them.

THANK GOD

MAVERICK CITY MUSIC

fourteen
WALKING IN FAITH

For we are co-workers in God's service; you are God's field, God's building.

1 CORINTHIANS 3:9

THE NEXT STEP in construction is choosing what flooring will be installed in the house. There are many choices: wood, laminate, tile, carpet, or a combination of them. It can depend on the room and personal preferences. Laying down flooring includes learning what is needed to prepare for each choice. How we choose to walk out our faith will include how we serve others. It will take practice to listen for God's voice in where and how we will serve. When learning any new skill, we need some preparation and practice. For example, when writing a book, it takes practice and time to get to that finished product.

Preparing the floor starts with making sure it is level. Sometimes it will be just you and God working on re-leveling your priorities, such as how you spend your time. It is in that preparation work when you may learn what your next steps in your personal journey of how to serve God will look like.

Once the preparation is done, it's time to install the flooring. I have been able to help lay a couple of types of flooring: tile and laminate. One of the important things in laying tile is the spacers between the tiles for the grout. For tile, you want those gaps, but with laminate, gaps aren't good as it means you didn't interlock them correctly. With both, it's almost impossible to fix any crookedness or gaps once they are set. Thankfully, although our walk of faith may not be a straight road and may have gaps, God walks with us every step.

Many years ago, I took my parents to the Royal Gorge Bridge in Cañon City, Colorado. It is the highest suspension bridge in the United States. Some planks were close together, but some had a bigger gap where you could look down and see the ground far below. It was scary. Similarly, in our faith, we have to keep our eyes up to God and not down to fear. The story of Peter stepping out of the boat and walking on the water to Jesus is a great example of this. When he kept his eyes on Jesus, he was ok. But when doubt sank in, so did he.

The best example of walking out your faith through service is Jesus washing the disciples' feet. "He got up from the meal, took off his outer clothing, and wrapped a towel around his waist. After that, he poured water into a basin and began to wash the disciples' feet, drying them with the towel that was wrapped around him" (John 13:4–5). He led by example, showing what servanthood looks like. It can mean getting down and dirty. Feet washing is one of the most humbling things I can think of to do. This was done at the Last Supper, which means he took the time to serve others just hours before he was crucified. Serving others takes a conscious effort from us, but we also need God's help.

This story wasn't the first encounter the disciples had experienced of someone washing their feet. It was customary for a servant to wash the guests' feet as part of their purification process. As Jesus was at the home of a Pharisee for dinner, a woman, described as sinful, came with her alabaster jar. "As she stood behind him at his feet weeping, she began to wet his feet with her tears. Then she wiped them with her hair, kissed them and poured perfume on them" (Luke 7:38). That a sinful woman was touching Jesus appalled the host. But Jesus used this as a teaching lesson: because of her repentance, she was forgiven. Jesus then told her, "Your faith has saved you; go in peace" (Luke 7:50).

Paul used feet in connection to peace in his description of the armor of God: "And with your feet fitted with the readiness that comes from the gospel of peace" (Ephesians 6:15). We are called to let our shoes of peace, the peace of Christ, guide us on our faith walk. This shows us that once we receive the gospel, there is a deeper peace that can only come from God. This peace will increase our desire to be humble and serve more deeply.

Serving others will look different for every person. However, Jesus cautioned us against using service as a way to seek others' approval and applause. Instead, it is more meaningful to just have the moment between you and the other person, guided by God. Like Jesus said in the Sermon on the Mount:

> So when you give to the needy, do not announce it with trumpets, as the hypocrites do in the synagogues and on the streets, to be honored by others. Truly I tell you, they have received their reward in full. But when you give to the needy, do not let your left hand know what your right hand is doing, so that your giving may be in secret. Then your Father, who sees what is done in secret, will reward you. –Matthew 6:2–4

One example of humble service in the Bible was the boy with the loaves and fish. He didn't have much, but he offered what he had. When you read about how many people were fed, it was only the men who were counted, not the women and children. That means the boy who offered his meal wasn't part of the official count. Someone that didn't seem to matter to the world was the one who helped Jesus with the miracle. We can feel like our small gestures don't matter in the big picture, but it can mean the world to that person.

I have found that God has put people on my path for a reason. One day, while working in a medical office, a man on the other end of the phone was seeking more than just an appointment. We had a nice conversation about a variety of topics. Since we were on the phone for so long, it was clear he wasn't a patient and was simply in need of a friend. One comment that stood out was when he said, "You showed up for the need right now." I don't know what impact our conversation made for him in the future, but feeling connected with another person gave him hope. That summarizes what our faith should look like: to show up for what is needed, even if it is to listen and offer comfort. Those types of encounters will help build our faith. I don't know if that gentleman was a believer or not, but I can hope that it did build his faith, even if that faith was in the goodness of humanity.

Deciding to listen to God's call and serve others includes determining what sacrifices you are willing to make. At a recent Bible study I attended, we talked about agape love, the sacrificial love. Jesus showed us his agape love for us, first in the feet washing and then on the cross. The sinful woman and young boy both gave up what they had, showing their agape love in their own ways. The woman who was cleaning Jesus's feet wasn't even invited to that dinner, but she was where she needed to be, like the boy with the loaves and fish. We are often in the place God wants us to serve and need to be open to listening to those calls. Our walk may feel different at different points in life, like when we walk from one type of flooring to another. The most important lesson is we are called to walk the path of Christ.

REFLECTION QUESTIONS:
1. *How does being humble while serving help to build your faith?*
2. *Are you willing to take the time and do what is asked to prepare yourself to serve in the way God has called you?*

BUILDING CHALLENGE

Going back to the story of Peter stepping out of the boat, why was he the only one that stepped out? How are you willing to step out to serve others?

JESUS AT A DISTANCE
CASTING CROWNS

fifteen
FURNISHING REFUGE

> **God is our refuge and strength, an ever-present help in trouble.**
>
> PSALM 46:1

AFTER ALL THE major construction pieces are done comes the fun part: choosing furnishings—cabinets, beds, dressers, etc. This is when we make this house into a home, or what we can call a place of refuge, escape, rest. Your home should help give you the strength to walk your faith journey.

Another important part of building your faith is taking time both inside and outside of the home to listen to the quiet voice of God. But we have to make our home a place to find the peace of God. When I think of items in my home that give me refuge, a few of them are quite similar. First, my little blanket that I called, "Bankie," that I would cling to for comfort as a child. Next, a small quilt my aunt made that has pigs all over it. I love pigs and can remember when the quilt helped me feel safe in a thunderstorm in Minnesota. And third, a prayer shawl that I clung to many nights in the past few years. The shawl has a metal cross stitched in, and I would trace it as I fell asleep. All these items helped shield me from the world and point me back to seeking refuge in God. They helped me feel the love of others and God.

The second lesson is finding inspiration in the items you choose to have in your home. I don't consider myself an interior designer at all. However, when we decided to remodel our kitchen, I think we did a pretty good job. We kept the flooring and most of the appliances. We decided to refinish the cabinets, so, in theory, it was much simpler than a complete redo. What took the longest was sanding and staining all the cabinets. That meant many tedious hours of concentration, but as we finished each section, we could step back and look at the progress we'd made. When it came time to choose a countertop, we took pieces of each element—tile, backsplash, and cabinet door—to the store. I felt like I was on one of those shows on HGTV where they pick coordinating items. Once it was all completed, I felt calm and excited at the same time. What I mean by that is I felt peaceful and inspired to keep trying new things. Isn't that what we want from our faith journey as well?

The third lesson is to not let the goal of accumulating items take over our peaceful residence. One of the most freeing projects can be to purge a closet, a dresser, or a room. When we did the kitchen remodel, I spent time going through each cabinet and drawer, deciding whether we still wanted each item inside. Some things we had never used, or it had been several years since we had used it. It was so refreshing to declutter. It can be easy to keep accumulating items without even realizing it. These items can be a barrier to our relationship with God. Remember the story in the Bible about the man who wanted to build a bigger barn to store his grain so that he wouldn't have to worry about anything? God replied with, "You fool! This very night your life will be demanded from you. Then who will get what you have prepared for yourself?" (Luke 12:20). The lesson was that the man put his selfishness and greed over God. You can take the opportunity to give those excess items to someone else.

The fourth lesson is to seek places outside the home that help you connect with God. While there, you can let your mind and heart be more open to what God might be telling you. For me, spending a few moments in nature, such as going camping in the mountains or sitting on the beach, can be a great escape. In Michael and Jon Haley's book *I Must Go: An Epic Journey of Knowing God and Finding Purpose*, they describe the highs and lows of hiking the John Muir Trail. They shared how we all seek "mountain-top experiences" where we feel God's presence. We can't stay on the mountain, but we can share what we experienced on that mountain with others. We can also access those memories when we are in the valley or just the routine of life to remind us how God is present with us at all times. They compared muscle memory to faith memory. Our muscles get stronger the more we use them, and the same can be applied to our faith. "Maybe your faith is weak simply because you haven't exercised it in awhile."[1] The solution can be to find moments with God, even if it requires our physical muscles to help build our faith muscles.

One way to stretch yourself is to decide beforehand to put your focus on God during those getaways. That may sound strange as it doesn't seem spontaneous, but the point is to be more intentional in those moments. One way I have challenged myself to do this is to connect Scripture to the nature around me. For example, when seeing green pastures or a lake, I remember, "He makes me lie down in green pastures, he leads me beside quiet waters" (Psalm 23:2). I also try to take pictures of both God's beauty and more simple things, like muddy footprints, and then reflect on what I can see in those shots. Next, because we are called to share moments to inspire others, I share them on social media. I know social media gets a bad rap for all the commotion and dissent, but I use it to encourage and inspire others. We have access to many forms

---

[1] Michael Haley and Jon Haley, *I Must Go: An Epic Journey of Knowing God and Finding Purpose*, Fort Worth, TX: Independently Published, 2020, p. 27.

to express ourselves, but it is important to remember that we show our love towards God in those expressions.

The final lesson is a somewhat misunderstood story in the Bible that refers to finding rest: "'Come to me, all you who are weary and burdened, and I will give you rest. Take my yoke upon you and learn from me, for I am gentle and humble in heart, and you will find rest for your souls. For my yoke is easy and my burden is light'" (Matthew 11:28–30). What is misunderstood is the word "yoke." The definition of yoke is "a wooden crosspiece fastened over the necks of a pair of oxen or horses. The yoke was connected to a plough, cart or wagon so that the combined force of the two animals could be evenly distributed."[2] If we are yoked to Christ, we will find rest. How does that make sense? It means that if we let Jesus lead us in our walk, we can find peace. Jesus takes on our burdens, if we let him. I have found this to be true in my writing journey. When I wasn't writing, I felt disconnected and distant from God. But the time I spend writing and talking about my journey gives me a boldness that only comes from God. "If we are not stretching our faith by taking steps in our walk that do scare us a little, then we really

---

2   Oxford Reference Online, s.v. "yoke (n.)," accessed on December 23, 2023, https://www.oxfordreference.com/display/10.1093/oi/authority.20110803125349876?d=%2F10.1093%2Foi%2Fauthority.20110803125349876&p=emailASZV7t6w2WTVA.

aren't walking by faith."³ The lesson is to declutter what is blocking you *from* God, whether it's belongings, time, or focus, and seek those moments of refuge *in* God.

REFLECTION QUESTIONS:
1. What is an item or two of refuge in your home that reminds you of God's love?
2. How can you find rest in Jesus?

BUILDING CHALLENGE

Go on a walk or drive and see what Scriptures you can tie to your surroundings.

---

3   Michael Haley and Jon Haley, *I Must Go: An Epic Journey of Knowing God and Finding Purpose*, Fort Worth, TX: Independently Published, 2020, p. 74.

PART THREE
Living

sixteen

WHO IS INVITED TO COME IN?

Beloved, let us love one another: for love is of God; and every one that loveth is born of God, and knoweth God. He that loveth not knoweth not God; for God is love.

1 JOHN 4:7-8, KJV

As the completion of the house is getting close, there is a question to address: who are you welcoming into your life? The list starts with your family, your church, your place of employment, and your friends. Are you holding on to certain traditions because that's where you feel comfortable? Or are you willing to build your faith by hospitality? The Greek translation of hospitality is "love the stranger." Are you open to welcoming those who have different lifestyles from you, or is your heart needing to be expanded?

One movie that I watched many times as a child was *Fiddler on the Roof*. I watched it again more recently and had a greater understanding and respect for the story and the struggles that the characters faced. "The main theme of the movie is that without their religious traditions, the lives of Jews 'would be as shaky as a fiddler on the roof.'"[1] One of the main characters, Tevya, begins the story with the song "Tradition." As he tries to maintain Jewish traditions, life around him is changing. I can relate. Change is challenging and unknown. The Jewish people have been tested throughout the generations, or as one of my favorite lines from Tevya states, "I know we are the chosen people. But once in a while, can't you choose someone else?"[2]

The answer to Tevya's question came in the New Testament: Yes. God shows us that all who believe Christ died for our sins are included (chosen) in the Kingdom. This is illustrated in the story of Peter. Peter was challenged on that shaky roof by a vision of all kinds of animals, reptiles, and birds. "Then a voice told him, 'Get up, Peter. Kill and eat'" (Acts 10:13). Peter refused because he had never eaten anything unclean. This repeated three times, then the vision ended. He was then invited to the

---

[1] *Fiddler on the Roof* FAQ, IMDB online, "What is the fiddler? What does he represent?" accessed on November 5, 2023, https://www.imdb.com/title/tt0067093/faq/.

[2] Norman Jewison, dir. *Fiddler on the Roof*, United Artists, 1971, viewed via DirecTV.

home of Gentiles, who had been guided in a vision to seek Peter. Peter admitted it was against the Law for him, a Jew, to visit a Gentile. But, because of his vision, he said, "But God has shown me that I should not call anyone impure or unclean" (Acts 10:28). His experience helped build the church of the Gentiles, who are now included in the promises of God.

This inclusion of non-Jews should not have been a surprise to the apostles as Jesus had already shown them examples of loving the stranger. He showed mercy to the Samaritan woman and healed many people far away from Jerusalem. As a final instruction, Jesus gave the apostles the Great Commission: "Therefore go and make disciples of all nations, baptizing them in the name of the Father and of the Son and of the Holy Spirit, and teaching them to obey everything I have commanded you" (Matthew 28:19–20).

In one Bible study class I attended, Jesus's call to us was referred to as "radical discipleship." If we truly want to follow Jesus, it means that we will be in situations where we are called to "love the stranger." It may mean we go on a mission trip in another country, but more likely, it will be serving the people in our own community, our neighbors. Loving our neighbor includes our place of employment, our own family and friends, and those in our church. If we can be an example of Jesus's love in our own circle, it can have a rippling effect into the world, like a stone skipping across the water.

"Loving our neighbors is not the same as simply not hating

them. Love is not a lack of hate or of anything else. According to Scripture, love has form and content and it compels us to act. It compels us to actively seek the well-being of others."[3]

Sometimes it may feel like we're on an extremely different path than another, but like Paul wrote:

> Consequently, you are no longer foreigners and strangers, but fellow citizens with God's people and also members of his household, built on the foundation of the apostles and prophets, with Christ Jesus himself as the chief cornerstone. In him the whole building is joined together and rises to become a holy temple in the Lord. And in him you too are being built together to become a dwelling in which God lives by his Spirit.
> –Ephesians 2:19–22

My Bible commentary described these verses like this:

> Are we spiritual construction projects? Prior to the resurrection, many believed God's glory could only reside in the Jerusalem temple. But Paul said that the church—made up of God's people—is becoming God's new residence. The construction work isn't finished yet.

---

[3] Clergy Coaching Network, "Loving our neighbors is not the same as simply not hating them," Facebook, August 13, 2023, https://www.facebook.com/photo/?fbid=668813055278337&set=a.547725677387076.

That's why it's described as both a present reality and a future goal.[4]

What I like about this commentary is how the church is both the present and the future, and we all have the opportunity to show the glory of God to others. We can show hospitality not only with family and friends, but in our workplaces too. As Christians, it is also important to show compassion with people you don't know. You may be the only person to show them Jesus through actions and words. "The only thing that counts is faith expressing itself through love" (Galatians 5:6).

It is easy to say that you know you should show hospitality, but it's in the doing that you build your faith. Jesus used the parable of the separation of the sheep and the goats to show how we will be judged when the Son of Man comes in his glory (Matthew 25). Those who will receive their inheritance will be those who fed the hungry, invited in a stranger, clothed the naked, cared for the sick, and visited the imprisoned. The people in the parable were confused as to when their King had those needs. He replied, "Truly I tell you, whatever you did for one of the least of these brothers and sisters of mine, you did for me" (Matthew 25:40). While this parable may be describing how people in the Tribulation will be judged, it is a challenge to all Christians to show compassion to others.

---

4   *NIV Quest Study Bible*, Grand Rapids, MI: Zondervan, 2011, p. 1736.

It can be easy to show hospitality to someone of high esteem, but Jesus challenges all of us to reach out to those we may consider least, including the homeless, prisoners, and those with disabilities. Wouldn't it be great if everyone in the world would try to do that more? Unfortunately, we live in a broken world, and believers need to step out of our comfort zone and be guiding lights to the broken. All people are God's creation. Let's try to break the tradition of not just staying with people we are comfortable with, but showing Jesus more in the world.

REFLECTION QUESTIONS:
1. How can you show more love in your own circle of people?
2. How can you show more hospitality and let in new people into your life?

BUILDING CHALLENGE

Find a faith-based organization in your community that serves one of the following: homeless, imprisoned, widows, orphans, or other marginalized groups. Take the time to go volunteer to show Jesus in the world.

THE COMMISSION

seventeen

DELAY'S OR GOD'S TIMING?

Although I hope to come to you soon, I am writing you these instructions so that, if I am delayed, you will know how people ought to conduct themselves in God's household, which is the church of the living God, the pillar and foundation of the truth.

1 TIMOTHY 3:14-15

WHEN IT COMES to any project in construction, it is vital to allow time for setbacks and delays. If you've watched any of the home improvement shows, you know they set a short timeline to get all the projects done. They invariably run into problems, like needing new wiring or leaks. Somehow, with the magic of TV, they complete it in their set number of days. In real life, there are many times when a project or time of struggle seems to stretch out.

It may even feel like the blessing is just beyond our reach and requires our faith to be stretched.

Most people are familiar with the story of Joseph and his multicolored coat. He was the favored child of Jacob and Rachel, and his brothers were jealous of him. It didn't help that he shared dreams he had about them bowing down to him. When his brothers had a chance to get rid of him, they took it. They plotted to kill him but then had a better idea to sell him as a slave to a caravan coming by. He was taken to Egypt and enslaved in the home of Potiphar, who was one of Pharaoh's guards. Joseph earned Potiphar's trust and ran his household. However, Joseph was accused of trying to sleep with Potiphar's wife and thrown in jail. His position went from bad to worse. Or did it? He won the favor of the warden, who put him in charge of the other prisoners. He then was able to interpret other people's dreams.

Thankfully, when Pharoah needed a dream interpreted, one of Joseph's former prison mates remembered him. Joseph helped interpret the dreams, which, in turn, gained the Pharoah's respect. The dreams prophesied an upcoming famine, so Pharoah gave Joseph charge of the land of Egypt and their food supply. Because of the dreams and their correct interpretations, the Egyptians had time to prepare. In God's plan, Joseph's brothers came to Egypt during the famine, looking for grain. Can you imagine all the emotions Joseph had when he saw his brothers? He was excited to see his own family, but only after he had found the strength and peace to forgive them.

When Joseph revealed himself to them, he said, "And now, do not be distressed and do not be angry with yourselves for selling me here, because it was to save lives that God sent me ahead of you" (Genesis 45:5). Wow! Joseph could see how God had worked in his life, all the twists and turns, for the good of his people, including his own family. In a sermon I heard about this story, it was pointed out how God was with Joseph through it all. It didn't mean that he didn't go through trials and valleys, but that God was with him there too.

One interesting observation in this story is that the genealogy of Jesus doesn't go through Joseph. Instead, it's his brother Judah. But if Joseph hadn't been there to plan for the famine, Judah and his family wouldn't have survived. Sometimes, it may feel like you are not doing something big for the Kingdom, but it may be that you're helping another complete their calling.

Joseph appears to have been a born leader, but it took years of preparation and faithfulness to God. We may have a dream we want to pursue, but it also has to be in God's timing. I can relate to a lot of what Joseph went through. When I felt the real push to write, it had been over twenty years since I had written in my journal about publishing. If you had read one of the papers I wrote in college, you would have questioned my writing abilities. Then, I had many years of quiet where I did not feel the inspiration and motivation to achieve this dream. I was building my faith in other tasks I felt led to do.

Then, right after my first book came out, one of the first questions I received was, "Are you working on a second one?" I said yes, as I already had the idea for this book, but I also felt the pressure rise to hurry and get it done. When I didn't feel the inspiration to write, it felt like a setback. Even though it was what I felt was my calling, I needed to take the time to build my faith more.

One lesson came as I was editing my first book. I was challenged to come up with my own publishing name as I was self-publishing. That sounds like fun, but I struggled. I tried to think of something clever, but everything I came up with, someone else had beat me to it. One Sunday, I was determined to figure it out. I went for a walk with contemporary Christian music blaring in my ears and tried to focus on this task. I got home, thinking I had it, but once again, someone else had beat me to it. I then started to text my pastor a rant about how I couldn't figure it out when it hit me. Had I asked God for the name? The word *ask* kept repeating in my mind. Then, I thought of Matthew 7:7:

> "Ask and it will be given to you; seek and you will find; knock and the door will be opened to you."

Those three words—Ask, Seek, Knock—spelled ASK. That was it. It sounded so simple, but it can be so easy to forget to ask. It starts with asking, but then requires us to seek and knock. Even though I wanted to rush to finish this second book, I needed to wait for the right timing. I also had to seek the right words from God. Then, when I felt the timing was right, I began writing.

Waiting for the right time can look a lot like patience. In a world of immediate gratification, the concept of spiritual building goes against the grain. It may feel like God is silent, but it is more likely that God is seeing how you handle the time of waiting. You are not alone in this area as many people in the Bible besides Joseph had to wait for God's timing. Abraham waited for the promise of generations to come from his line, and Jacob waited years to marry Rachel. Even Jesus had years where all the Bible states is, "And Jesus grew in wisdom and stature, and in favor with God and man" (Luke 2:52). In these times of waiting, keep building by studying, praying, and serving.

Even though it may feel frustrating to have setbacks or delays in your life, know that God is with you in it all. And don't give up on your dreams. I want to end this chapter with a prayer and praise of God's timing: "LORD, you are my God; I will exalt you and praise your name, for in perfect faithfulness you have done wonderful things, things planned long ago" (Isaiah 25:1).

REFLECTION QUESTIONS:
1. When did a time of waiting help you trust God's timing?
2. What dream would you like to complete or achieve?

BUILDING CHALLENGE

ASK!

eighteen

GROWING FAITH

> **Love is not some small minded ideal that we bypass on the way to weightier theological principles. Love is PhD-Level Christianity. In our pursuit of Jesus, we will spend the rest of our lives learning to love more passionately, intimately, intentionally, and transformationally. There is no higher call.[1]**

ONE THING TO consider is leaving room to expand and/or grow your house. It can include an addition, a garage, or garden space. When it comes to your faith, how are you growing in what you are called to do? How

---

1 Clergy Coaching Network, "Love is not some small minded ideal that we bypass on the way to weightier," Facebook, October 12, 2023, https://www.facebook.com/photo/?fbid=703267421832900&set=a.547725677387076.

has God been preparing you for your calling longer than you may have realized?

Your calling is using the gifts of the Spirit with God's guidance. "We have different gifts, according to the grace given to each of us" (Romans 12:6). It can be tempting to compare ourselves with someone else because they have a gift that we don't. But, like the parts of our body have different functions, we can appreciate everyone was given a different set of talents. We also can show our love for others and God through the unique gifts we've been given.

Some people are called to tell others about their experiences through writing and speaking. Writing has been where I have found joy. It also has pushed me to trust God more deeply. Like a garden, my roots have strengthened while facing the weeds (insecurities and fears). It's a work in progress, like we all are. I had known since I was a teenager that I wanted to publish, even putting a goal of two books in my journal. What has gone along with writing is also opportunities to speak about my faith journey. After publishing my first book, the marketing side was a steep learning curve. I never had an interest in marketing, but it's amazing how God will put that drive in you to do things you never imagined you could do. I was and still am introverted, but when it comes to my calling of writing, I get a boldness that comes from God.

When I think back to how God has been preparing me for this part of my journey, I can go back to the drama class I took in high school. I chose the class because my sister Jen was into theatre, and I wanted to be like her. One of the group scenes I participated in was from *Steel Magnolias*. If you know the movie, you know the line, "Knock her lights out, M'Lynn!"[2] That was my line. I was responsible for the twist in the scene and had to get the words out right for the full impact. Little did I know then that a class like that was preparing me for the speaking opportunities I have been given now. The perfectionist in me wants to get those words just right, like in the scene. But I have a hidden weapon when I speak about my faith: the Holy Spirit. I used to have to write out exactly what I wanted to say in my meditations I gave as an elder at my church. Now, I have word prompts and allow the Holy Spirit to guide my words.

One of the messages that the Holy Spirit has spoken to me to give is "You are not alone." God has shown me areas in my life where I have felt alone, including my writing journey, mental health struggles, and burnout. He then brought people into my life who have dealt with the same issues. It connects us, and we can now support one another through it. In my first book, I wrote about how I struggled in the transition of looking for a new job after leaving an unhealthy one. A friend of a friend reached out to me, asking if I could call her. She shared she was looking for a job and knew I had some experience in that from reading my first book. We talked about

---

2 Herbert Ross, dir. *Steel Magnolias*, Tri-Star Pictures, 1989.

being open to different experiences, but I also talked about how God was showing me areas where I am not alone. Her response was, "I didn't know I needed to hear that." That's the power of the Holy Spirit. We think we know what we want, but we do not always know what we need.

The Easter morning story is a great example of not getting what you want, but getting what you need. This story is summarized in a children's book I got in the mail called *Run and Tell!* The children's book explains that the women went to the tomb to finish the burial traditions. First, the women were told by an angel that Jesus had risen and is alive. They were told to run and tell the others. Peter and John, when they heard the news, went running towards the tomb. Finally, Mary Magdalene got to see the risen Jesus and went quickly to go and tell the others. The women and the disciples who went to the tomb were mourning the loss of their friend and teacher. Their mourning quickly changed to a joy much deeper than they could have ever conceived.

Jesus also turned their calling from just being his followers into being some of the first people to tell others about the risen Christ. Our calling can morph into something more if we are willing. Like in the parable of the servants who are given gold, those who were able to double their investments were told, "Well done, good and faithful servant! You have been faithful with a few things; I will put you in charge of many things" (Matthew 25:21). If we choose to be obedient in using our gifts, our calling may expand further than we can imagine.

What also stands out in this story is how they ran. Not walked, not sauntered, instead, they ran. They wanted to share the Good News as soon as possible. We can all use this sense of urgency in our faith journeys. It can be tempting to think we have all the time in the world to share our faith with others. "When you run, focus on Jesus (the way) and not the race."[3] The important thing to remember is to use the boldness of the Holy Spirit to guide you when you speak and what you say. I know a lot of people who have said they wouldn't know what to say, so they don't do it. But this is where we can grow in our calling and faith with the guidance of God.

Everyone's calling and gifts look a little different, and that's a good thing. We can meet the needs of others with our own unique skills and abilities. "Each of you should use whatever gift you have received to serve others, as faithful stewards of God's grace in its various forms" (1 Peter 4:10). Keep your heart open, and God will show you where you are called to serve.

---

3 Bishop Emmanuel Klufio, "When you run, focus on Jesus (the way) and not the race," Facebook, April 8, 2023, https://www.facebook.com/photo/?fbid=710417124417734&set=a.130992602360192.

BUILDING FAITH

Reflection Questions:
1. When did you get what you needed, not what you wanted?
2. What are your spiritual gifts? If you can't identify them, ask God to show you.

BUILDING CHALLENGE

Welcome (and don't run from) any expanding roles God is giving you.

nineteen

GLAD TO BE HOME!

For we know that if the earthly tent we live in is destroyed, we have a building from God, an eternal house in heaven, not built by human hands.

2 CORINTHIANS 5:1

IT'S FINALLY TIME to celebrate on move-in day! It is the completion of all the choices you've made in your life. It included some setbacks, twists, and turns. It also means you are leaving the old place you've been living, which can be bittersweet. Thankfully, if you are a believer, this is what we are all striving for: to be in heaven with God.

Life can feel like a race in which you are always chasing goals and dreams, but also grinding away in daily activities. One show that I have enjoyed watching is *The Amazing Race*, where teams of two race around the world, completing challenges and navigating to the next clue. I enjoyed it so much that my husband and I have pretended to be on the show a couple of times while catching public trains. The first was when we were in Atlanta with family as we navigated back to our hotel. My husband and I were the winners of that race leg.

God used that show to motivate a friend and me to pick up our pace while transferring trains in Germany. My husband yelled, "We're on *The Amazing Race*! Come on!" After hearing little English for days, besides amongst ourselves, we heard, "*The Amazing Race* is here!" To the German bystanders' disappointment, it was just Americans practicing their racing skills.

This life on earth flies by so fast. It's important to have people in your life who are encouraging and pushing you to run the best race you can. Unlike the show, where the slowest team is eliminated, we want as many people to run this race with us and make it to the finish line of heaven.

Running any race requires stamina and endurance. It takes proper care of our physical bodies as well. That includes proper nutrition, activity, and sleep. I know I am more determined to run my race when I feel my best. It can be hard if you have obstacles and hurdles that try to slow or stop you from your goals. Running the faith race is nothing new. As Paul wrote:

> Do you not know that in a race all the runners run, but only one gets the prize? Run in such a way as to get the prize. Everyone who competes in the games goes into strict training. They do it to get a crown that will not

last, but we do it to get a crown that will last forever. Therefore, I do not run like someone running aimlessly.
–1 Corinthians 9:24–26

Our goal should be: aim for the crown that will last forever.

The result of our endurance, our reward, is "an inheritance that can never perish, spoil or fade. This inheritance is kept in heaven for you" (1 Peter 1:4). We don't know what our new home in heaven will look like, but Jesus gave us some glimpses. He knew that this life on earth would have its struggles, but he gave us something to look forward to:

> "Do not let your hearts be troubled. You believe in God; believe also in me. My Father's house has many rooms; if that were not so, would I have told you that I am going there to prepare a place for you? And if I go and prepare a place for you, I will come back and take you to be with me that you also may be where I am. You know the way to the place where I am going."
>
> Thomas said to him, "Lord, we don't know where you are going, so how can we know the way?"
>
> Jesus answered, "I am the way and the truth and the life. No one comes to the Father except through me."
> –John 14:1–6

That's the gospel in a nutshell. Follow Jesus. It's good to be reminded of this often; we can lose focus on what's important.

Heaven is someplace I would love to go, and hope you do too. What a time of celebration that will be! There will be a lot of singing, dancing, and Hallelujahs, which means "Praise God!"

Until Jesus calls us home, we are called to keep building faith, in ourselves and others. "But you, dear friends, must build each other up in your most holy faith, pray in the power of the Holy Spirit, and await the mercy of our Lord Jesus Christ, who will bring you eternal life. In this way, you will keep yourselves safe in God's love" (Jude 20–21, NLT). That includes showing glimpses of heaven to other people. How do we do that? Keep striving to love God, others, and ourselves better. That is how we strengthen our faith day by day.

"Surely your goodness and love will follow me all the days of my life, and I will dwell in the house of the LORD forever" (Psalm 23:6).

REFLECTION QUESTION:
1. *How can you show heaven on earth to someone today?*

BUILDING CHALLENGE

Keep running and finish strong!

HEAVEN CHANGES EVERYTHING
BIG DADDY WEAVE

www.ingramcontent.com/pod-product-compliance
Lightning Source LLC
Chambersburg PA
CBHW071352080526
44587CB00017B/3069